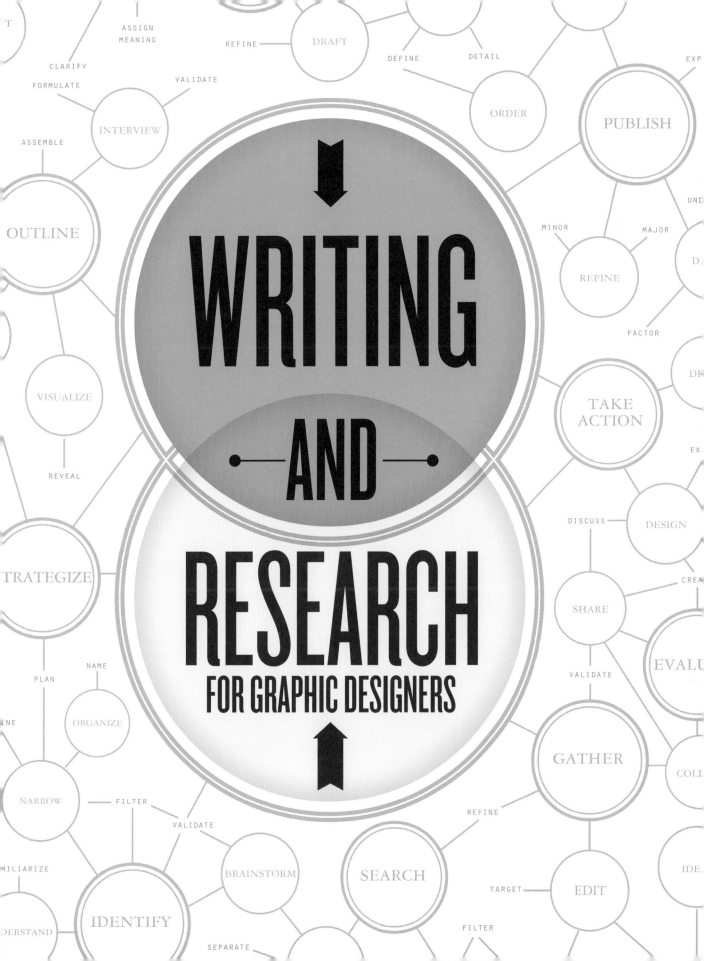

© 2012 Rockport Publishers
Text © 2012 Steven Heller

First published in the United States of America in 2012 by
Rockport Publishers, a member of
Quayside Publishing Group
100 Cummings Center
Suite 406-L
Beverly, Massachusetts 01915-6101
Telephone: (978) 282-9590
Fax: (978) 283-2742
www.rockpub.com

Library of Congress Cataloging-in-Publication Data

Heller, Steven.
Writing and research for graphic designers : a designer's manual to strategic communication and presentation / Steven Heller.
  pages cm
ISBN: 978-1-59253-804-1 (pbk.)
1. Commercial art—Marketing. 2. Graphic arts—Marketing. 3. Business writing. 4. Research. I. Title.
NC1001.H465 2013
808.06'6741—dc23

2012014787
CIP

ISBN 978-1-59253-804-1
Digital edition published in 2012
eISBN 978-1-61058-649-8

10 9 8 7 6 5 4 3 2 1

Design: Landers Miller Design
Cover Image: Landers Miller Design

Printed in China

STEVEN HELLER

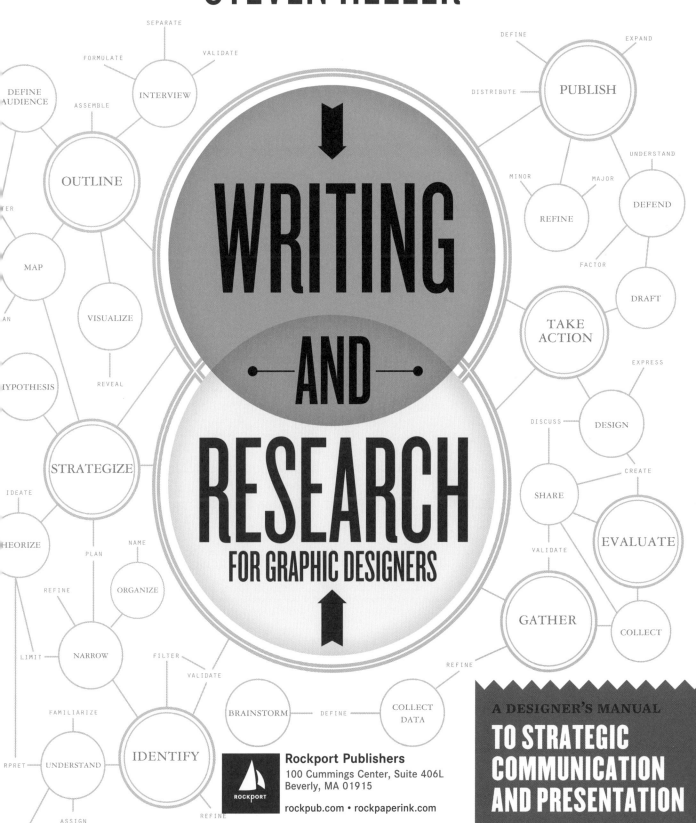

WRITING AND RESEARCH

FOR GRAPHIC DESIGNERS

SEPARATE
FORMULATE
VALIDATE
INTERVIEW
DEFINE AUDIENCE
ASSEMBLE
OUTLINE
MAP
VISUALIZE
HYPOTHESIS
REVEAL
STRATEGIZE
IDEATE
THEORIZE
PLAN
NAME
REFINE
ORGANIZE
LIMIT
NARROW
FILTER
VALIDATE
FAMILIARIZE
BRAINSTORM
DEFINE
COLLECT DATA
UNDERSTAND
IDENTIFY
ASSIGN MEANING
REFINE
CLARIFY

DEFINE
EXPAND
PUBLISH
DISTRIBUTE
UNDERSTAND
MINOR
MAJOR
REFINE
DEFEND
FACTOR
DRAFT
TAKE ACTION
EXPRESS
DISCUSS
DESIGN
CREATE
SHARE
EVALUATE
VALIDATE
GATHER
COLLECT
REFINE

Rockport Publishers
100 Cummings Center, Suite 406L
Beverly, MA 01915

rockpub.com • rockpaperink.com

A DESIGNER'S MANUAL

TO STRATEGIC COMMUNICATION AND PRESENTATION

CONTENTS/

1

PART ONE

READING
The Key to Good Research and Wrting

PART TWO

WRITING
Thoughts on Paper or Screen

PART THREE

RESEARCH
Building the Narrative Foundation

2

⬛ : CASE STUDY

⬤ : Q & A SIDEBAR

ACKNOWLEDGMENTS

I cannot thank enough my Rockport editor, Emily Potts, for her continued encouragement and expertise. She has long been an enthusiastic cheerleader, yet a hard taskmaster. Thanks also to Winnie Prentice and Regina Grenier at Rockport for all their support, especially on this project.

Kimberlie Birks, my former SVA MFA D-Crit student, contributed much to the early stages of this book. Thank you for your great spirit and assistance. Rick Landers, my former SVA MFA Designer as Author + Entrepreneur student, has been the design backbone of many books I've written and edited over the past decade. His great eye and sound judgment are essential to the success of these projects.

To David Rhodes, president, and Anthony Rhodes, executive vice president, of the School of Visual Arts, I am very grateful for all the incredible support I've received for this and other activities.

Thanks to all the writers and editors who have enriched my life and made important contributions to this book: Alice Twemlow, Rick Poynor, Ralph Caplan, Veronique Vienne, David Barringer, Allan Chochinov, Akiko Busch, Deborah Hussey, Aaron Kenedi, Phil Patton, Sue Apfelbaum, Adrian Shaughnessy, Andrea Lange, Liz Danzico, Maria Popova, Michael Grant, Gail Anderson, Kerry William Purcell, Ellen Shapiro, Linda King, Sean Adams, Alissa Walker, Michael Dooley, and Jude Stewart. Tips of the hat to archivists Beth Kleber at SVA and Alexander Tochilovsky at Cooper Union for their words of experience.

Also, it is with much appreciation that I acknowledge the designers who contributed their word/image confections to this book: Andrew Byrom, Seymour Chwast, Paula Scher, Stefan Sagmeister, and Stefan Bucher.

To my colleague and co-chair at MFA Design/Designer as Author + Entrepreneur, Lita Talarico, I thank you for such a long and fruitful collaboration.

And finally, all my love and thanks to my wife and collaborator, Louise Fili, who has entered her own world of writing and research with elegance and poise. And who always tries, often in vain, to keep me elegant and poised.

STEVEN HELLER

PREFACE
Designers, Meet the Word

Designers are routinely called upon to write about the images and designs they create. Writing and research skills are more necessary now than ever before—from basic business to advanced criticism. Writing about design is not just for the trade; it must be accessible to everyone with an interest in design.

Being able to express, analyze, and report on the issues of design practice demands facts, data, and research. Understanding how to turn information into valuable strategic assets is one of the key talents the design writer and researcher must possess.

This book is an introductory guide to various forms of writing and fundamental research—and how images can be visualized through words. It addresses communication on various levels and for multiple audiences: designers to designers; designers to clients; designers to the design-literate; and designers to the design-agnostic.

The methods of research discussed here include library, online, primary and secondary sources, and more. The methods of writing focus on trade journalism, scholarly and academic discourse, criticism, and general journalism, as well as fundamental business-to-business proposal and capability communications.

On what platforms can design research and writing be best distributed? This book focuses on magazines, blogs, papers, lectures, journals, books—and even press releases. And how can design, typography, and illustration be used in concert with good writing? You will see.

This is the first handbook for those designers who write and those writers who design.

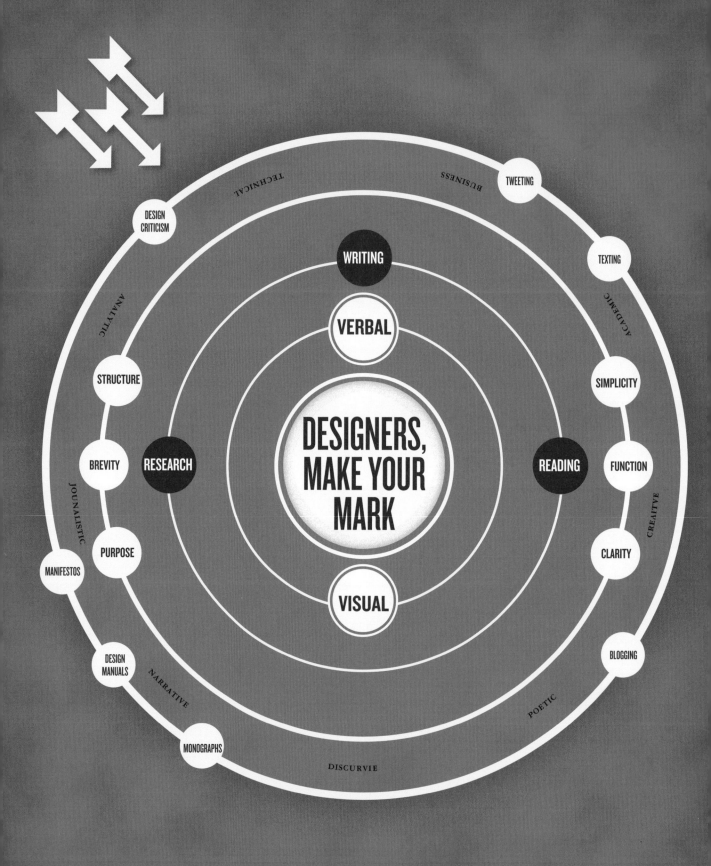

Toothless cowboys and whiskered prospectors—staples of classic Hollywood Westerns—could barely read or write, so they made crude marks in lieu of signatures. Graphic designers are not illiterate (or toothless) as a rule, yet according to a certain slander, they have been accused of not writing *or* reading. They only make marks—logos. Logic and a modicum of science hold that verbal, textual, and other cognitive deficiencies are precisely the reasons for becoming a graphic designer. If true, then to find a designer who can actually write *and* make marks is nothing short of miraculous.

In a word, nonsense!

So, let's bury this ridiculous fallacy on boot hill once and for all. Even if the stereotype held for a small minority who chose art school over a liberal arts college because they weren't adept "wordsmiths," any assertion that this is the norm is untrue. Right-brain/left-brain theories regarding visual versus verbal fluency are hardly definitive explanations as to why people do or do not become designers. Many visual people start careers as "artists," but an equally large number of writers join the designer ranks too. Writing is design.

Indeed, design "problem solving" requires many word and visual skills; how else can designers make those proverbial pictures that speak a thousand words? Often an image, glyph, or mark sparks as much understanding as any combination of words, sentences, or paragraphs—even more so. This accounts for why designing logos and trademarks is so valuable to business and so lucrative for some designers. Yet just as often, design is the frame that showcases words, and illustration illuminates them. Today, designers must master the visual and verbal. With increasing multimedia communication platforms opening all the time, reading and writing and, more than ever, research (a third imperative skill), are the designer's essential three R's.

It is not clear how the myth originated that designers (and illustrators) are as averse to reading and writing as old cowpokes and prospectors were to brushing their teeth. In fact, over the past two centuries designers have done a considerable amount of credible writing: everything from design manuals and manifestos to monographs and histories—and a few have published novels and screenplays too. Just because a graphic designer is expert at nonverbal expression does not mean she is verbally challenged.

On average, a graphic designer is, perhaps, not as skilled a wordsmith as the professional writer, but writing standards are relative—and quality can be improved through practice (as the old joke reminds us: *A man meets another on the street and asks for directions. Q. How do you get to Carnegie Hall? A. Practice!*). Designers do not write with the same frequency as they design, so they may lack a necessary level of confidence. But confidence is always fortified through experience. Akin to physical exercise, everyday writing tones up the intellectual muscles. One-two-three, one-two-three.

There are many ways to get exercise too. The rise of writing today can be ascribed to something even more fundamental: All designers work on computers, which are replete with keyboards. Like eating potato chips (it is impossible to eat just one), few people are immune to the allure of the keyboard pecking away and watching words emerge; the word faucet is hard to turn off once it starts flowing. What's more, designing in time and space with the employ of motion is now a significant and essential part of the graphic design skill set. Likewise, writing (and applying various methods of research) is integral to communicating on a multitude of old and new design platforms.

What is writing? Just pecking away is comparable to doodling. Serious writing demands structure, purpose, and function. There are many kinds of writing, from pro forma to expressive, from technical to narrative, from discursive to poetic. Whatever the form, writing is as essential to design as math is to science and science is to knowledge in general. Writing about design is a tool for collecting and disseminating knowledge. For now, however, we will focus on the basic essence of design writing.

Writing a simple coherent letter is an important business requisite; composing a cogent proposal for a job is essential. Clients want to be assured of fundamental intelligence and attention to detail (and with spell-check, there is no excuse for errors either). Fundamental writing expertise is valued as much as aesthetic and strategic design assets today. But writing today is also more challenging owing to the new standards and vernaculars. As early as grade school, abbreviation is an accepted means of formal communication. Facebook, Twitter, and messaging protocols have altered writing habits through shorthand and the introduction of new nouns and verbs into the language. While blogs encourage more writing and enable designers to share their thoughts and ideas with audiences, the inevitable informality, which can eschew rules of good writing and editing, results in poor language skills. Blogging, texting, and tweeting have produced new vernaculars rooted in abbreviation, which is not implicitly bad, but has impacted our forms of address. Nonetheless, language has always changed as customs do. Thank heavens, I pray thee, we doth speak any longer in Shakespearean English. Dig it, y'all gentlefolk.

Business-oriented writing—which does not have to be as strained as it often is—is but one type of writing. Designers are now called upon for a slew of different kinds of writing tasks, from academic to journalistic, critical to promotional, and more.

Designers must tell stories—they must ascribe narrative underpinnings to their designs or the work of others. Indeed, their designs must have a narrative. Context is everything, and writing helps establish the story that design wants to tell. Where once it was enough simply (and it is never simple) to make objects of design, now designers are encouraged to wrap their respective works in blankets of words that add an additional dimension to their output.

Writing about design (or writing about other things—art, politics, science—through a design lens) serves various functions. It is a means to explore and explain the intuitive qualities that often confound the nondesigner—and even the visually literate designer. Writing is a way to disseminate ideas and philosophies within design communities; a method of describing how work is conceived and fabricated; a vehicle to shed critical and analytical light, and provide transparency; and an ability to simply introduce all kinds of audiences to design. How can a profession as ubiquitous and encompassing as graphic design be taken seriously without a body of literature?

The difference between design writing and general writing is ostensibly nil. Yet all professional writing is prone to shorthand or jargon, and the job of the design writer is to use as little of it as possible. Even those in the know would rather read smartly constructed, flowing and entertaining prose than insider-speak. Design writing should respect the reader by not talking up or down—do not assume ignorance, but do not take knowledge for granted either. Balance is key.

Following rules is essential too. But rules of writing are often fungible. It is important to understand the end user's capacity for understanding. For example, avoid adding extraneous verbiage when writing for business outcomes, such as press releases or proposals of any sort. All writing can benefit from brevity, but business writing should stick to the point—hit the nails hard—without indulging in personal quirks. Creative writing, on the other hand, which involves developing narrative, should be as robust as possible, but never confusing. Writing, like design, benefits greatly from good editing (self-editing and that of professional copy editors). Avoiding what is turgidly or overly written requires the same judgment as knowing what's overly designed. Damn the adjectives! Damn the ornament!

Editing one's own writing can be difficult, even for seasoned writers. Yet for designers, editing design is second nature. For the untutored writer, editing words may demand greater forethought (writing a few drafts does wonders). While a good designer instinctually rejects unnecessary design elements, a good writer will avoid, for instance, florid prose. But here is the "takeaway": The insecure writer will throw in as many adjectives or adverbs or descriptors as possible to compensate for a lack of experience. In an effort to make text sound serious, the insecure writer is compelled to gild the lily. Although it is no longer miraculous that a designer can design *and* write—and read and research—that is not to say that it comes naturally either. Nor should it.

Another important piece of advice is, *Play to your strength!* This is one of life's mantras that need repeating. So, if writing is not your strength, exercise that part of your brain so that it can become more muscular. Try this: The more you read, the larger the pool of examples to build upon. The more you write, the greater the opportunity to try those examples to determine what works best. Don't be afraid to make mistakes. We all do. Copy editors—the writer's best friend—will usually fix the errors, and some will even teach the author why it was a mistake. With writing there is always a safety net as long as you don't fall madly in love with any single part of your prose. Words are free—and there are lots of them, so use them freely. The worst thing a neophyte or seasoned writer can do is to reject an editor's suggestions.

So why should you read this book? What will be your takeaway? This is both a guide to and a celebration of design writing and research. It is aimed at inspiring and instructing.

As a guide, the book features various authors and editors who have been asked to discuss writing and research in general and the genesis and progress of specific writing examples. The process differs from writer to writer and editor to editor—and this will be discussed.

As a celebration, the book's goal is to advocate for more design writing that illuminates the methodologies behind design "objects" that have distinct places in the cultural fabric. Writing and researching is design!

Whether you become a writer after reading this book is up to you. But you will doubtless appreciate that writing and research is an integral part of the design experience. If you become more adept at writing and research in part, then you have, in fact, started to make your mark(s) in the best way possible—as a visually and verbally literate designer.

Why *do* I write? I write, therefore I am. I need the intellectual and emotional stimulation that the act of putting down ideas in the form of words on paper and screen gives me. Writing is the culmination of a process of conceiving, researching, analyzing, ordering, and structuring. Writing is design.

So it makes sense that I write mostly about design.

As a kid, I thought I wanted to be an historian. My uncle, a former Columbia professor of American studies, taught me the pleasure of studying history. I loved reading historical tomes (especially about the Civil War and The New Deal), yet I had little patience for the rigors of academics. I was never a very good student. So I compensated for my scholarly deficiencies by writing and drawing. Indeed, I once handed in an illustrated paper on "isms," which was entirely plagiarized from a text that was, predictably, familiar to my teacher (at least he hadn't written it; now that would have been embarrassing). I received an F for the paper, but he gave me an A for the satiric artwork. It was a wash.

This act triggered an epiphany. My pictures were visualized words, and if I could conjure my own images, I could also write my own words. Although I didn't bother to rewrite the "isms" paper to get a better grade as my teacher suggested, I did begin to do more original research and write more original prose for subsequent history assignments. I wrote incessantly and took uncanny enjoyment in rereading my own words aloud to myself. I wanted to get the rhythm right. The one thing I missed, however, was a real focus for my writing.

Every writing teacher says to write what you know. Passion is the ticket to success. And my particular passion was for art, but not just any art: I favored the satiric kind. But not just any satiric art either; rather, the radically strident political commentary that shot barbs at fat cats and besotted cows, images that were caustic and indelible, like Goya's stern "Disasters of War." I found my initial métier was writing about how satire fought folly (and sometimes won).

As fate would have it, all those pictures paid off. When I was twenty-four, I was hired as art director of the *New York Times* Op-Ed page. Years before I began, that valuable real estate opposite the editorial page was already a revolution in journalism and journalistic illustration. Its visual personality was built on a foundation of satiric art history, and in order to do a credible job, I delved into the study of the eighteenth

1

century English master satiric printmakers William Hogarth, James Gillray, and Thomas Rowlandson; the nineteenth century French caricaturists Honoré Daumier, J.J. Grandville, and Gustave Doré; the American Thomas Nast; and finally the twentieth century Germans George Grosz, Otto Dix, and John Heartfield.

My method of learning, retaining, and refining what I learned was to curate exhibitions of work that interested me. I'd write essays for the exhibition catalogs, which I'd eventually expand into books. My first two full-bore exhibitions, at Goethe House and Alliance Française, respectively, in New York, were devoted to *Simplicissimus*, the acerbic late nineteenth century German satiric magazine, and *L'Assiette au Beurre*, the startlingly graphic French equivalent. I reasoned that these periodicals and the amazing work contained therein, attacking the mores and morals, religions and monarchies, and society and culture of their times, were the basis for contemporary graphic commentary—the kind that appeared on the Op-Ed page. Instead of simply filing away the knowledge I was gathering in the back of my brain, I wrote numerous articles about my discoveries. The artists I learned about were touchstones for more detailed commentaries about current practitioners. I learned as I wrote.

The old chestnut that knowledge is a tree with many branches is true. While researching satiric art, I'd climbed different limbs full of wonderful discoveries. The principle satiric artists I was interested in, it turned out, were also graphic, interior, and product designers and that led me to write about design. Finding that Bruno Paul, for instance—one of the sharpest graphic wits in Germany—was also a respected advertising poster artist, furniture designer, and head of a major design school in Berlin was a revelation. Learning that John Heartfield—the "inventor" of satiric photomontage—was also the art director and typographer at The Malik-Verlag, a communist book publisher in Berlin, was eye-opening. Discovering that Lionel Feininger—creator of the comic strip *The Kin-der-kids*—was one of the founding Bauhaus masters, was extraordinary. The connective tissue between art and design by artists who had been passed over by art historians became a rich mine of material for many of my essays for many years.

Mainstream art history had been pretty well mined, but with this new vein of historical material, I could keep prospecting for years—and I have.

Nonetheless, I am not a trained historian, and chronicling history has never been my sole interest. I have no desire to devote years or decades to one specific individual or topic (even though I've authored two professional biographies). My curiosity is just too broad and attention span too limited. So I turned to popular culture as my "beat" and have been writing, among other things, about contemporary designers and illustrators for more than a couple of decades. Focusing on their respective influences on the zeitgeist, I find many of their lives to be ready-made narratives, the best of which are models for others in the field. More important, I use their individual stories, in part, to alter the stereotype of "trade" journalism.

With notable exceptions, most design writing, from the early to late twentieth centuries, aimed at providing a professional audience with news, views, and tips. There was

Rethinking
Design II:
*The Future
of Print*

❶ Magazines then and now. *U&lc*, a
tabloid type journal, was platform
for many design writers.

❷ Rethinking Design. Mohawk Paper
Mills sponsored a critical journal,
edited by Michael Bierut.

❸ Gebrauchsgraphik, the German
advertising and design magazine
is a valuable resource for the
contemporary design historian.

❹ Eye, Edited by John Walters,
is a steadfast chronicler of the
new and old in graphic design.

EMIGRE NO.51 SUMMER 1999 PRICE $7.95

FIRST THINGS FIRST MANIFESTO 2000

We, the undersigned, are graphic designers, art directors and visual communicators who have been raised in a world in which the techniques and apparatus of advertising have persistently been presented to us as the most lucrative, effective and desirable use of our talents. Many design teachers and mentors promote this belief; the market rewards it; a tide of books and publications reinforces it.

Encouraged in this direction, designers then apply their skill and imagination to sell dog biscuits, designer coffee, diamonds, detergents, hair gel, cigarettes, credit cards, sneakers, butt toners, light beer and heavy-duty recreational vehicles. Commercial work has always paid the bills, but many graphic designers have now let it become, in large measure, *what graphic designers do*. This, in turn, is how the world perceives design. The profession's time and energy is used up manufacturing demand for things that are inessential at best.

Many of us have grown increasingly uncomfortable with this view of design. Designers who devote their efforts primarily to advertising, marketing and brand development are supporting, and implicitly endorsing, a mental environment so saturated with commercial messages that it is changing the very way citizen-consumers speak, think, feel, respond and interact. To some extent we are all helping draft a reductive and immeasurably harmful code of public discourse.

There are pursuits more worthy of our problem-solving skills. Unprecedented environmental, social and cultural crises demand our attention. Many cultural interventions, social market-ing campaigns, books, magazines, exhibitions, educational tools, television programs, films, charitable causes and other information design projects urgently require our expertise and help.

We propose a reversal of priorities in favor of more useful, lasting and democratic forms of communication - a mindshift away from product marketing and toward the exploration and production of a new kind of meaning. The scope of debate is shrinking; it must expand. Consumerism is running uncontested; it must be challenged by other perspectives expressed, in part, through the visual languages and resources of design.

In 1964, 22 visual communicators signed the original call for our skills to be put to worthwhile use. With the explosive growth of global commercial culture, their message has only grown more urgent. Today, we renew their manifesto in expectation that no more decades will pass before it is taken to heart.

Jonathan Barnbrook Nick Bell Andrew Blauvelt Hans Bockting Irma Boom Sheila Levrant de Bretteville Max Bruinsma Siân Cook Linda van Deursen Chris Dixon William Drenttel Gert Dumbar Simon Esterson Vince Frost Ken Garland Milton Glaser Jessica Helfand Steven Heller Andrew Howard Tibor Kalman Jeffery Keedy Zuzana Licko Ellen Lupton Katherine McCoy Armand Mevis J. Abbott Miller Rick Poynor Lucienne Roberts Erik Spiekermann Jan van Toorn Teal Triggs Rudy VanderLans Bob Wilkinson

↑ *U&lc*. edited by Margaret Richardson, encouraged its writers to write about new phenomena and old trends.

← *Emigre* magazine, opened the door to the most inventive experimental typography of the digital age. Here is the premiere of *First Things First*, a controversial manifesto from 1999.

little criticism in the form of serious analysis. It may have been thought that shinning a bright light on contemporary work would diminish or harm it (unless, of course, it was unquestioning praise). Yet other arts had a long tradition of critique—if only as consumer "reviews"—so why shouldn't design in general, and particularly graphic design, have a critical language? The real challenge was determining what vocabulary was appropriate—and accessible. Many of the arts have been insulated from public discourse through self-referential jargon (architecture is a prime example). I felt that following the theoretical convolutions could relegate graphic design writing to an arcane footnote.

Yet rather than ignore theory, I simply chose to refrain from spouting excessive academic newspeak (I even curtailed the use of words like modality, taxonomy, and paradigm). I decided the best approach was a transparent writing style that is accessible and entertaining.

I employ various methods, but the one I most enjoy (and if I enjoy it, maybe the reader will too) is building narratives directly from the voices of my varied subjects. The key is linking quotations together through the glue of descriptive and discursive prose. Making sure there is a narrative arc at all times; starting out strong, settling down, building up, and ultimately packing the finale with solid idea, making for a satisfying read. I'm pretty good with segues from paragraph to paragraph, but always have trouble with endings. I'm grateful when, at times, the stories actually write themselves from start to finish.

My biography of Paul Rand (titled *Paul Rand*) was such a book. Written as a series of essays, the book features chapters that are held together through commonalities in ways that surprised even me. Rand's story was so compelling, the quotes I used directly from him and others who knew him were so evocative, and the anecdotal material was so illuminating, I couldn't fail as long as I didn't mistakenly erase the entire manuscript.

In 2010, I completed a professional biography of Alvin Lustig (*Born Modern: The Life and Design of Alvin Lustig*), a designer from the same period as Rand, who left behind a wealth of letters and notes. Sadly, he passed away in 1955 at age forty, so unlike Rand, I never met nor interviewed him. His detailed letters, however, chronicled the professional and personal aspects of his life almost as well as, if not better than, face-to-face encounters. The letters allowed me to engage his voice; then I filled in the gaps with reporting and commentary. I don't always enjoy being the neutral narrator, but in this case it was appropriate—and pleasurable.

All writers have an insatiable need for gratification, so pleasure is the supreme perk of writing. The process of writing, the act of editing and being edited, and then the ultimate climax—the publication, the rereading and reflection—this is *Why I Write*.

READING

WRITING   RESEARCH

Which comes first, reading, writing, or research? Learning to read usually precedes learning to write, although in primary school the two go hand-in-glove. Research is a more sophisticated process, learned later in life. Presumably the readers of this book already know how to read and write, and most have done what can be called research. So, where these three activities intersect, however, may be the pertinent question.

Here's a theater analogy: Reading sets the stage. Research provides the cast. And writing is the performance. If this seems strained, it is not – just think about it. Without good reading habits, research will be superficial at best. Research results in the information, data, anecdotes—the content—that writers must have to tell a story. Without something to say, there is nothing to write about. So, these three activities are integral parts of our play—and yet they are also self-sufficient.

One can read and not write. One can write and not research. But the end product will be doubtless lacking. This may sound obvious, even sophomoric, but whatever the analogy, it is essential that if one wants to be a writer, the joy of reading and the skill of research must be harmoniously practiced. A good writer will learn from reading and benefit from research, and that's the truth.

READING
The Key to Good Research and Writing

Some people, these days, read only Twitter or Facebook feeds. From this statement you may anticipate a grumpy lament like the current "reading is dead" canard. But I am not entirely a grump, and this book is far from a lament. Nonetheless, my assertion is quantifiable. Long-form thoughtful reading is down; short-form speed-reading is up. Still, the good news is that any form of reading implies literacy. The bad news is that speed-reading clogs the brain with minutiae and TMI (too much information).

Reading and writing go hand in glove. Sure, it is possible to read and never write an essay, article, or book in your life, but it is impossible to write anything and never read. A philosopher named Theodore Parker (1820–1860) would have agreed: "The books that help you most are those which make you think the most. The hardest way of learning is that of easy reading." Another venerated spokesman for reading, John Locke (1632–1704), noted: "Reading furnishes the mind only with materials of knowledge; it is thinking that makes what we read ours."

Some of those old guys stole our best ideas, type master Frederic Goudy wrote more than a hundred years ago, so we should listen to what they say.

Certainly, media has transformed, mutated, and multiplied since the seventeenth and eighteenth centuries when dinosaurs such as Locke and Parker roamed the earth, but their notions about reading are still valid. Reading is, as a copywriter wrote for

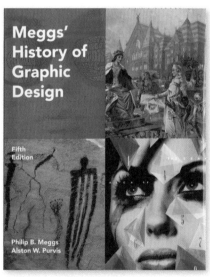

↑ *Meggs' History of Graphic Design*, was the first formally written history textbook.

❶

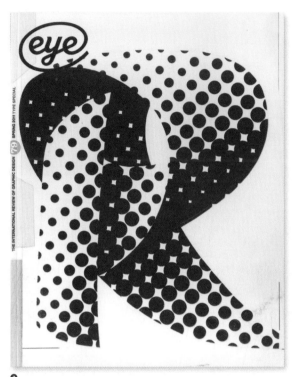

❷

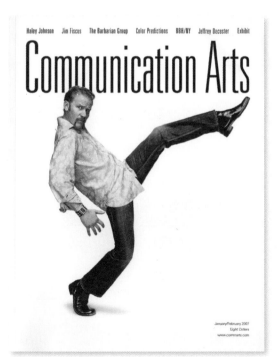

❸

❹

an old public service TV commercial, "fundamental." It is not enough to read only captions in a visual book. The text is there to be read too.

While it is perfectly allowable to skim or glean information from a text, actually reading an article or a book from beginning to end is ultimately a more pleasurable and cognitively valuable experience. Yet whichever way one chooses to read—front to back, back to front, middle to wherever—the goals are the same: enjoyment and knowledge.

Yet this is a quid pro quo situation. If an author gives you those pleasures, as a writer you should be able to return the favor—or strive to do so—for others. Reading provides models. Since different writers work in varied styles, it is likely that reading a variety of authors will add to your skill set: Some of their approaches will inform your own proclivities. I am not advocating blatant copying. But if the shoe (or approach) fits . . . well, borrow techniques that will allow for the most expressive flexibility. Writing is about finding a voice. Personality is key, but structure is essential. Reading others' work can help build the foundation for that structure.

Reading should not be a chore. But it can be a muscle-toning exercise. Reading other writers' work invariably triggers one's own writing. Emulating another writer is as valuable (and flattering) as enjoying his text, and is sometimes unavoidable.

What to Read

In the fictitious twenty-fourth century, as a respite from seeking out new worlds, *Star Trek's* Jean-Luc Picard sits in his captain's seat with a rare, leather-bound relic in his hand. Despite predictions to the contrary, the book in the future is still viable (at least in science fiction). Yet as boundless as it may be, the definition of a book may demand revision. Digital "readers" are making inroads and the iPad is the future. Yet even in the most futuristic science fiction projections, the book continues to hold a place of honor.

You are reading this book (and have gotten this far) because you want to write about design. So, in addition to reading your favorite fiction and nonfiction, poetry and verse, how-to and self-help, children's and young adult, as well as newspapers and magazines in whichever media you choose—in print or

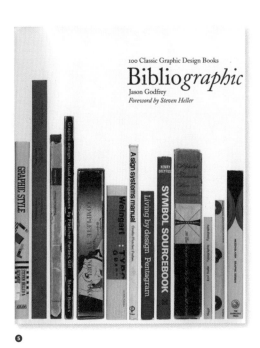

5

What to read influences how to write. Here are four of the leading design magazines known for smart writing and exciting design.

1 *IDEA* from Japan serves a regular diet of international news and features.

2 *Eye* from the U.K. balances graphic, motion and dimensional design with a strong leaning toward history.

3 *Communication Arts* from the U.S. has long advocated the interdisciplinary side of graphic design.

4 *Print*, the oldest running graphic design magazine, views popular culture through the graphic lens.

5 *Bibliographic*, is a survey of 100 of the most significant graphic design text and picture books. Although not the canon, it comes close to being the optimum reading list.

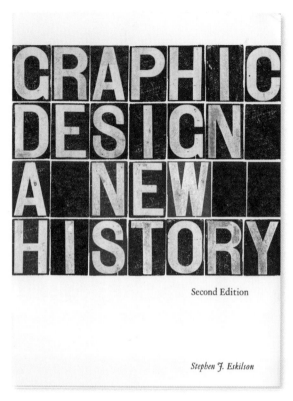

↑ *Graphic Design: A New History* proves that there are many ways to write about design history.

on Kindle, iPad, or Nook—you should also read some design writing (including the case studies in this volume).

You might, however, want to start with design history as your grounding in the field. Just three decades ago there was not a single tome devoted to the history of graphic design. Then, in 1983, Philip B. Meggs (1942–2002) published the first edition of *A History of Graphic Design*. His premier work chronicled the first image (Lascaux), first printing press (Guttenberg), and first typefaces (Latins), and provided the first accepted taxonomies for Western graphic design movements and styles. His book was adopted as the primary history text and stood alone for more than ten years. In 1994, Richard Hollis's *Graphic Design: A Concise History* appeared, offering a more digested but no less insightful account of the early, orthodox and post-modern legacy. A few supplementary histories were also published, including my own *Graphic Style: From Victorian to Post-Modern* (1988), coauthored with

Seymour Chwast, and *Nine Pioneers in Graphic Design* (1989) by R. Roger Remington and Barbara J. Hodik. Each cut the pie a little smaller. *Graphic Style* (now in its third edition) looked at the continuum of changing style and *Nine Pioneers* analyzed American design through its leading form givers. That was it for more than a decade.

It never rains, but it pours. Commencing in 2004 a publishing deluge began. The French poster historian Alain Weill published *Graphic Design: A History*, a slim book that summarized much of the same ground as Meggs and Hollis. Two years later, in 2006, another accomplished French design historian, Roxane Jubert, published *Typography* and *Graphic Design: From Antiquity to the Present* in English and in French, which covered much the same material, but also uncovered historical ground from a European perspective (like sign lettering during the German occupation of France). A year later, in 2007, Stephen J. Eskilson's *Graphic Design: A New History*, a hotly debated book that, while covering much the same turf as Meggs, Hollis, and Jubert, saw graphic design through an "art" historical lens (an expanded second edition was published in 2012). In 2009, Johanna Drucker and Emily McVarish's *Graphic Design History: A Critical Guide* was released, following a more traditional textbook format and focusing on how technologies altered design—it is also whittling away at Meggs' hold (the fifth edition published in 2012) on textbook dominance. That same year, *Graphic Design, Referenced*, by Armin Vit and Bryony Gomez Palacio, was released as an encyclopedic collection of brief design history facts. Just when it appeared—at a time when the graphic design history publishing

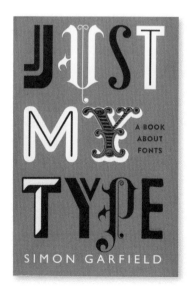

Just My Type is a witty romp through the world of "fonts" for both the insider and outsider.

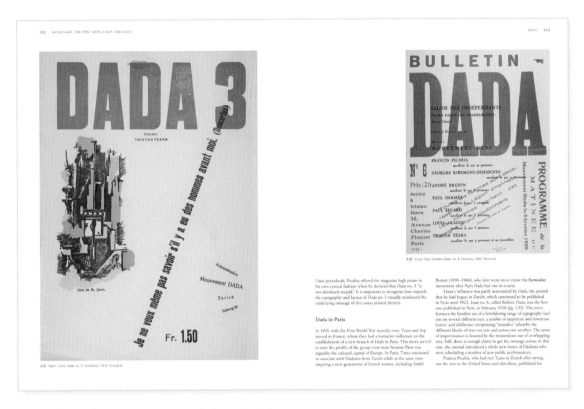

⬆ A spread on the Dada movement from *Graphic Design: A New History*.

market couldn't be any more saturated—along comes *The Story of Graphic Design* by Patrick Cramsie in 2010.

One telling of history was enough? Despite variations in voice and perspective, are there not only so many ways of carving up the pie without redundancy? These omnibus books have been written and rewritten, so who needs another graphic design history book? Frankly, we all do. I believe the field is all the richer for distinct viewpoints and new discoveries.

In addition to these histories, essay anthologies are edited samplers of design thinking and commentary from various writers. There are many such books in and out of print, but single- and multiple-authored books from Allworth Press, Princeton Architectural Press, and Yale University Press, to name a few of the leading anthology publishers, will give the neophyte writer a balanced selection of styles and methods—and an assortment of different styles and voices.

Illustrated design books are too often designated "eye candy," and while a number of them serve as pictorial records, most are inspiration for other designers, and therefore are essential to design practice and cultural study. An excellent book on design books is Jason Godfrey's *Bibliographic: 100 Classic Graphic Design Books*, which collects and comments on many of the key texts and monographs.

While most graphic design books are usually produced for a professional or student audience, even this should not be a stigma; many such books are reliquaries of popular culture—and appeal to wider audiences (whether they know it or not).

As your reading list grows, let's not forget vintage (and antique) books. They are rich repositories of design knowledge as relevant today as they were when first published. *Seven Designers Look at Trademark Design* (1952), edited by Egbert Jacobson, may survey the work of designers such as the late

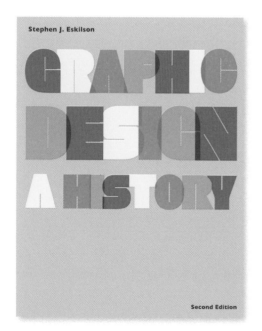

↑ The Second edition of *Graphic Design: A History*,
enabled the author to fix the mistakes and
add material that was subsequently researched.

Paul Rand, Herbert Bayer, Will Burtin, and Alvin Lustig,
but in some cases the logos are still extant and in others they
provide valuable case studies in success and failure. *Graphic
Design: Visual Comparisons* (1959), written by Alan Fletcher,
Colin Forbes, and Bob Gill during their pre-Pentagram days,
is a collection of disparate yet corresponding images that is as
inspiring for young designers now as it was for the young back
when it was published.

Who doesn't like to read magazines? Over the past couple
of years, a few important graphic design magazines in the
United States and abroad have folded or severely reduced
their pages. A once bountiful field of design publications is
migrating to digital formats. Although a few old standbys
are still plugging away, the successful magazines cannot
resist digital pressures, and new digital outlets, such as Design
Observer (http://designobserver.com), are wellsprings of writing.

Graphic design magazines, such as *Print*, *Communication Arts*,
Eye, *Idea*, and *Baseline*, as well as academic journals including
Design Issues and *Culture*, are evidence of the development of
styles, propagation of standards, and canonization of the profession. Although current periodicals have come a long way since

the late nineteenth century periodicals, the common editorial mandate to report, analyze, critique, and showcase contemporary and avant-garde achievement is what makes these journals integral to the study and practice of graphic design.

How to Read

All of us read sequentially—in the West usually from left to right. But we also read in spurts, jumping from line to line, paragraph to paragraph, and page to page. We are torn between this phrase and that idea. Our media are print and screen, with more of the latter coming into play. There are, perhaps, too many options today. Attention is compromised every time we click on a hotlink, or turn a printed page and remember something we forgot or need to do. We have to learn how to read again, especially if we want to write. We must become reacquainted with the sublime solitude of spending time absorbing the static page. Letters and words need not take flight or ring-a-ding to make us take notice. Reading is receiving information in a contemplative way.

Learning (or relearning) how to read means changing habits. If you are a skimmer, slow down. If you are a fragmenter, take in more. If you are a multitasker, focus on one medium or a single text, if only for a finite time frame. If you read in a linear, thoughtful, and absorbing way, well, then, good for you.

Where to read is also part of this equation. Be comfortable, but not excessively relaxed. Don't lie in bed or on the couch, like a slug. Sit up straight, preferably at a desk or in a chair. Unless you are reading before bed in order to fall asleep, your mission is to stay awake and be productive. Slow down, but don't drift off.

Taking Notes

One way to apply the brakes, to absorb more, and to focus intently is to take notes. Whether they are detailed or in shorthand, underlined or highlighted, or on sticky notes or notepads, jotting down or making extensive notes will be beneficial over time. (I routinely find marginalia made long

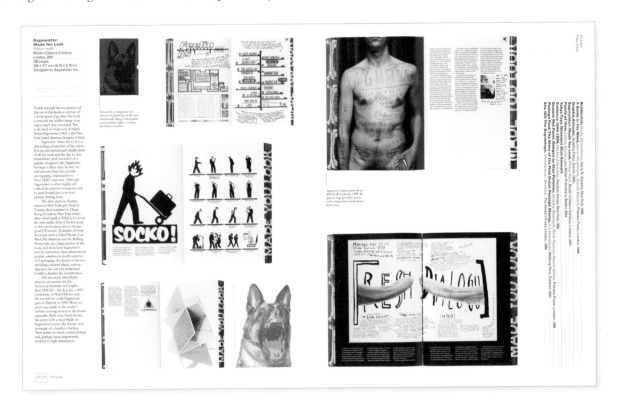

ago that prove invaluable, and congratulate myself for having such foresight.) Note taking also puts the brakes on your subconscious. Rather than lightly skimming over the surface, you are forced to pay attention—and maybe even read the same passages more than once. And don't fret about defacing a book or magazine. Sure, don't write notes in priceless antiques, but don't feel inhibited by any other media.

Note taking is an art in itself and demands organizational skill. One way is to jot down references in the margins or on separate pages. This works fine but does not help you cross-reference your notes to your readings, when you want them. Instead, write notes on index cards or in a book or on your iPad. Make sure you include citations that enable you to refer to the page, paragraph, or section of what you have been reading. If inputting notes into your laptop, you might also tag the notes, giving them thematic keywords. You can always introduce customized codes that only you will decipher, but depending on your method—analog or digital—you can find what you need quickly and efficiently. Clear and concise note taking is an investment in time that you'll never regret.

Reading offers two obvious rewards. First is seeing how others write. Sampling mannerisms, styles, structural forms, and more will allow you to test your own abilities and determine a comfortable writing technique. Second, of course, is information. There are various ways to research and develop content, and reading is fundamental in all of them.

Once you have established good reading habits, you are just about ready to write on your own and, with practice, in your own voice.

← *Design Observer*, the most widely read of all the design blogs.

THE DESIGN OBSERVER GROUP   DESIGN, CULTURE, CHANGE

HOME

OBSERVATORY

  CHANGE OBSERVER

 PLACES

 OBSERVER MEDIA

 OBSERVERS ROOM

 W

Books + Store   Sponsor

Paula Scher

All Maps Lie

Map of Midtown Manhattan from the book *Maps* by Paula Scher

In the late 1950s, when I was eight and nine years old, my father spent his weekends in the basement of our small, single-story house, measuring and cutting up pieces of light green laminated board. My mother repeatedly admonished my brother and I not to bother him because he was busy constructing an important invention. My brother and I continuously made fun of the so-called invention because it appeared to be nothing more than a piece of cardboard with three holes cut into it. We would describe to each other the scraps of board lying around with the cutout holes and break out into a gale of laughter.

I knew that my father was something called a "civil engineer" and that it was different from being an engineer on a train. I was told that he was a special kind of engineer and that his specialty was photogrammetry. I couldn't actually say the word, or explain what photogrammetry was, until I was an adult. A photogrammetric engineer studies the science of cameras. My father worked on aerial photography in the mapping division of the U.S. Geological Survey.

My father called his invention Stereo Templates. The three perfectly positioned circles that were cut into the light green laminate board functioned as a measuring device that helped correct the distortions in blown-up aerial photographs used for mapmaking.

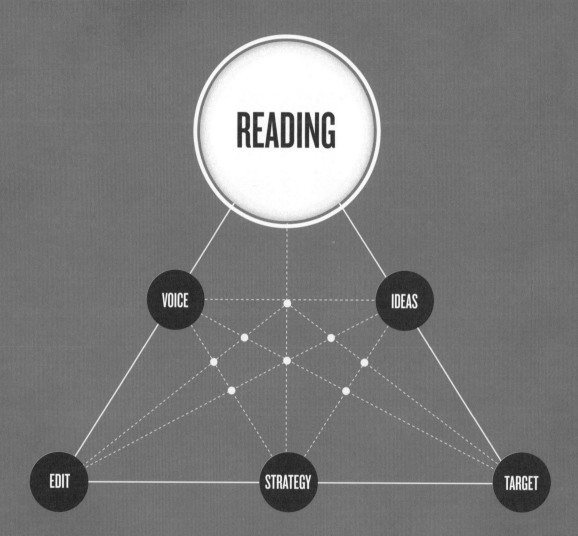

WRITING
Thoughts on Paper or Screen

Getting your ideas across is a big job. Taking your thoughts and translating them into written language is not to be taken lightly. This section will provide the tools you might need. But first, get in the mood.

Where you write is as important as how you write. What is the most comfortable place to be? For me it is in a comfy office chair in front of a large screen; if it is less than 33 inches (84 cm) I feel constricted. So find your comfort zone—whether it's a desk with writing paper, a lap with your Mac Air, a table with a large keyboard, or even one of those things . . . what is it called? Oh yes, a typewriter. Make sure you are away from distractions too. No phones. No open web pages or apps. That being said, everyone has rituals. Figure out what yours are and get them out of the way.

When I start a new essay or article, I have to walk around the room a bit before I achieve my first paragraph. Then I have to release all the clichés I know on the page or screen. Once they are written and then edited out, I'm ready to start. That's when I being to really exercise my voice.

Your Voice

There is writing and then there is WRITING. Almost anyone can write a note or letter. Putting words together that result in a comprehensible sentence is not terribly difficult once you acquire the knack. Making those sentences fit neatly into a paragraph, however, is exponentially harder. Then from one paragraph to a string of contiguous paragraphs that tell a story or convey a layered message, now that is difficult. That is what many call writing.

What I call fundamental writing is in all lowercase in the previous paragraph, because it is by no means extraordinary that a designer can successfully master this skill. Even if visual literacy is your forte, verbal literacy—and that means transcription of thoughts and ideas through words—is essential to being a designer. You have to know how to read and write to graduate from any school, including the design academy.

On a scale of one to ten, just being proficient at lowercase writing is a five. This means you can write a common letter, convey instructions, maybe even pen a proposal or brief for a particular design. To rise above that baseline, however, you must also have a voice. By voice, I mean personality. And by personality, I mean a quality of putting words, sentences, paragraphs, and thoughts together that are noticeably your own—some method or manner that distinguishes what you have to say, and how you say it, from standard or proper usage. This can be accomplished in any number of ways.

Where Ideas Come From
by Ellen Shapiro

Ellen Shapiro is a graphic designer, blogger, and author.

Half of my articles were assigned by editors. Sometimes I knew very little about the design firm, illustrator, or photographer I was asked to write about. So a journey starts that begins with research and proceeds to visits and interviews. That's the fun part.

Writing, like design, can take you into places you'd otherwise never have the opportunity to experience.

Most of my larger, trend pieces are instigated by me. Target is doing some of the most interesting retail and product design in the country and making (fashion, interior) designers the stars of the show. The new United Airlines campaign uses top illustrators from all around the world with "Rhapsody in Blue" as the theme song. A whole design team in Beijing, China, a country without a design tradition (as we know it), is getting the biggest brand launch in history ready for the Olympics. I pitch those ideas to the editors. I pitch hard to sell the story. Those are my best articles because I'm passionate about them.

But there are fewer opportunities now. Magazines have tighter budgets and are publishing fewer issues per year, with shorter, less literate articles. Shall it be a blog post for $100? Not worth the trouble that all the research finding out the who, what, when, and why would take.

I like writing blog posts because they're immediate. I can see something today and it's posted tomorrow. The lead time for design magazines is forever, and stuff can be very old news by the time it's published. Writing for blogs is quite different: fast and personal. Unfortunately, due to the total glut of stuff out there, it's not valued very highly.

Your voice can be an ability to write fluidly, with relative ease. Following all the rules of grammar or not, allowing your speech patterns to guide your writing style, rather than unnaturally formatting what you want to say, you allow your conversational tone to appear on the printed page.

Alternatively, your voice can be rather formal. Dotting all your i's and crossing all your t's can result in a style that says you are in command of the English language and deliberate in what you have to say.

Sometimes achieving the more informal voice is as simple as using the first person; other times it involves injecting adjectives to add descriptive color. Usually, the formal voice is more in the third person void of an abundance of descriptions. But there are no fixed rules. In fact, if you follow too many rules you may drown out your voice.

Early in a writer's development there is a tendency to impose the self-conscious or strained voice. The right tone doesn't materialize overnight. It takes time to develop and mature. In fact, try different approaches to determine what is comfortable. Actually, there is no one correct tone or timbre. Some writing will be more serious. Having a sense of humor is great, but not always appropriate. So the voice should modulate based on the context. Often in the quest for the best voice, a writer will graft tones that are not really honest. Time is on your side. There are no deadlines, no demands. The voice or voices should evolve.

Write the way you design. If you are a generalist designer, unfettered by a specific style, then follow that method. If you have a particular visual or conceptual stylistic leaning, then your writing voice might echo that. If you decide your design and writing sides are best when they are separate, then you will find the essential balance. But just as you never design without purpose, never write without it either. Your writing should be informative, enjoyable, perhaps even entertaining. The role of the voice is to ensure that your content does these things, and more.

Getting Ideas

A voice is nothing if you don't have a solid idea to write about. Where ideas come from is probably the most frequently asked question by youngsters and oldsters. How do ideas materialize? How can you determine whether they are worthy of the time and effort spent on making them a story?

Some of your story ideas will come from the inner recesses of your mind, usually prompted by something you see, hear, or read. Sometimes this is called instinct. Often you are more viscerally sensitive to ideas that make interesting stories. If you have particular passions, they might translate well into story ideas. But frequently, an editor

To write strategically, it is important for the writer to read the reader.

will suggest an idea and you will have to make it concrete. The designer and writer Ellen Shapiro offers some thoughts about running with her ideas, and the limitations therein (see page 32).

Strategic Writing

There is a lot of talk these days about "strategic design" and "design strategies" with regard to developing systems for the future where designers can optimize their creative and manufacturing output for clients. One of the leading advocates of this approach is Tim Brown, CEO of IDEO. In a June 1, 2005 article in Fast Company, titled "Strategy by Design," he wrote, "People need to have a visceral understanding — an image in their minds — of why you've chosen a certain strategy and what you're attempting to create with it. Design is ideally suited to this endeavor. It can't help but create tangible, real outcomes." This is a clear statement, free from the motivational mumbo jumbo that has enthralled business leaders for decades.

Brown is an exponent of the concept called "design thinking" and his strategic texts are intended to bring this latest professional buzzword to light. "Organizations need to take design thinking seriously," he wrote in the same article. "We need to spend more time making people conscious of design thinking — not because design is wondrous or magical, but simply because by focusing on it, we'll make it better. And that's an imperative for any business, because design thinking is indisputably a catalyst for innovation productivity. That is, it can increase the rate at which you generate good ideas and bring them to market. Where you innovate, how you innovate, and what you innovate are design problems. When you bring design thinking into that strategic discussion, you join a powerful tool with the purpose of the entire endeavor, which is to grow . . . ."

These words are as compelling as they are illustrative of how strategic writing, published in influential venues, can build a base of adherents. But there is a tipping point in all motivational or manifesto-like writing where newly coined terms fall into jargon territory. For example, here is where the buzzwords, such as *innovate, empathetic,* and *T-shaped people,* are introduced:

"Regardless of whether your goal is to innovate around a product, service, or business opportunity, you get good insights by having an observant and empathetic view of the world. You can't just stand in your own shoes; you've got to be able to stand in the shoes of others. Empathy allows you to have original insights about the world. It also enables you to build better teams. . . .

"We look for people who are so inquisitive about the world that they're willing to try to do what you do. We call them 'T-shaped people.' They have a principal skill that describes the vertical leg of the T—they're mechanical engineers or industrial designers. But they are so empathetic that they can branch out into other skills, such as anthropology, and do them as well. They are able to explore insights from many different perspectives and recognize patterns of behavior that point to a universal human need. That's what you're after at this point — patterns that yield ideas."

Don't misunderstand me, Brown's logic is impeccable and his voice is clear. Whether or not I like the buzzwords, they have strategic muscle. I have long been suspicious of the term *design thinking,* believing that all designers think, so to separate it from quotidian matters is basically marketing-speak. But Brown explains the term in such a clear way that it does not sound like it is being used as a substitute for real thinking.

"Design thinking is inherently a prototyping process," he wrote. "Once you spot a promising idea, you build it. The prototype is typically a drawing, model, or film that describes a product, system, or service. We build these models very quickly;

Use your voice judiciously to bring your readers along with you.

they're rough, ready, and not at all elegant, but they work. The goal isn't to create a close approximation of the finished product or process; the goal is to elicit feedback that helps us work through the problem we're trying to solve. In a sense, we build to think."

I have not excerpted Brown's words simply to caution against using them, but rather to use them as an example of how to write well in this tricky strategic genre. Buzz must be balanced with intelligence. To write strategically, it is important for the writer to read the reader. Jargon only works when everyone is on the same page. The purpose of strategic writing is to get people to that page—and then up to speed.

Targeting an Audience

Before writing your first sentence, know exactly whom you are writing for. I am writing for designers, design students, and a growing number of design writers—some trained as designers, and others not. You are my core audience. So I presume that some of what I have to say is known to you already. The rest is what you are interested in. I know we have some common ground: the design language. So, as I write these words and reprint other authors' writing about design, I am confident that you will be able to grasp, with luck, enjoy, and most hopefully, learn from the content offered to you.

Knowing your audience is not a Sphinx-like riddle. When setting out to write anything from a business letter to journalism to promotion, you must have the receiver in mind. You may not know the specifics of that person's reading habits, but you have a general understanding of what your reader finds interesting and will readily understand. Write to that knowledge.

If your audience is academic, they will expect a certain level of rigor. If they are commercial, then they have their own distinct criteria. Sometimes formality is required; other times an informal approach might be better. When I write for designers like you, I include details that the nondesigner might find arcane,

superfluous, or worse, boring. When I write for a broader public, I either eliminate the arcane material or make an effort to explain that material in layman's terms.

New writers sometimes include too much detail in their writing. It is a function of insecurity. Hint: It is usually better to write more than less, if only because it makes editing easier. More makes reduction and condensation considerably less of a chore. It allows the editor to determine what is really important. What's more, you should never take for granted that the reader knows what is in your mind. Retain enough information so that the reader feels secure that you are a confident narrator. Don't write down to your audience, but don't be too highbrow either. Balance is the key.

New writers also have a tendency to inflate themselves through bloviated prose. (Just the word bloviate is a kind of bloviating.) It is never necessary to show how smart you are in each sentence. Your intelligence—and more importantly, your authority—will come through sustained text that a reader will enjoy reading because the ideas are sound and the writing flows. If your encyclopedic mind is splattered all over your text, it will come off as such. If you modulate your content, your audience will learn better and retain more.

Leading your reader to the watering hole will come with experience. You don't want to get too far ahead of the reader, but you don't want to fall behind the reader's expectations. And remember, an audience—the reader—is not monolithic; your target audience has different levels of understanding, comprehension, and need. Use your voice judiciously to bring your readers along with you.

Self-Editing

Before you finalize a manuscript for your editor(s) to review, make certain it is everything you want it to be—take as much time as you need to self-edit.

Editing and rewriting is an integral part of the process. Nothing comes off the keyboard fully formed or spanking clean. I guarantee you will change your lead paragraph several times over the course of reading it back to yourself. (And it is a good idea to read it aloud to yourself to hear the cadence.) Lead paragraphs—yes, the ones you've worked so hard on and sweated over for so long—are routinely edited or eliminated. The first thing to tell yourself—and believe it too—is that every word, thought, or paragraph is expendable.

Self-editing is not always easy, because you have an investment in your words. Editors exist, in part, as a mediating force. They perceive what you cannot. But their existence does not obviate the importance of a thorough self-edit.

When writing, there is a natural tendency, even for the veteran writer, to include more verbiage than is necessary. For the neophyte, adding more adjectives and adverbs is like riding a bike with training wheels. At some point you have to balance yourself without the additional appendage. Some writers see self-editing as a process of elimination, removing all the extraneous matter (hopefully without losing the voice).

That precious lead paragraph you are so pleased with might really be "throat clearing" before getting to the point. Like a preliminary sketch, writing a lead paragraph may provide different alternatives or prove that none of your options are all that effective. Remember, there are probably various ways of saying the same thing. What you want is to pique the reader's attention. A good lead sentence or engaging lead paragraph will do that. But then there must be follow-through. Self-editing is an opportunity to determine whether you are succeeding. It is also insurance against repetition.

When self-editing, read your text as much for enjoyment as to fine-tune what you've done. Fewer acts are more satisfying than reading your own words expressing your own ideas. Warning: Don't allow the self-editing process to paralyze you. It is just as easy to get bogged down in elimination and reduction that results in chaos. Be judicious. Just prune enough to get to the point where your editor can take over.

The Editor's Role

"In the beginning God created the seas and the mountains. . .and then He created editors."

I'm almost certain my editor will want to remove the previous phrase for any number of valid reasons (one being that it is silly, arch, and strained). Still, my insistence will trump good editing, and the editor will be forced to leave it in (with this note left in the margin: "This is not worthy of you!").

Ⓠ/Ⓐ
Phil Patton Talks about How Writing is Editing

Phil Patton writes about design for the New York Times.

What is your editing process?

Writing is editing, almost all the way from the beginning. With digital media having replaced pen and typewriter, the first challenge is sequence. Concentrate on writing from beginning to end to get the skeleton of the story or argument. It is dangerously tempting to simply stack or arrange notes or comments and hope they will simply gel—that won't happen. Once you have the bones, you can add and cut. But no one can be one's own editor; get readers who come fresh to the page to give you perspective—roommates or strangers.

What do you do when editorially blocked?

When blocked, stop, back the bulldozer up, take a break, and then come back a few minutes or hours later, from a different angle. Walk or run or bike to let the process of writing and thinking go on as it will, in the background. Dickens daily strolled tens of miles across London while working on his novels and couldn't work if he couldn't walk.

The copy editor is more than a mechanic, responsible for tuning under the hood: He is the guarian of the written word.

The editor's role is not to scold, however. First and foremost it is to prepare the text for general consumption—which means, in part, taking out bad or mixed metaphors. The edited text should be as clean as possible, absent all the common grammatical and spelling mistakes, but also written so that the principal points are not buried under minor ones. It is the editor's responsibility to give your manuscript a good washing.

There are routinely a few editors that handle a manuscript meant for publication. Usually the editor who assigned the book, article, essay, or whatever gives it a once-over for meaning and sense. She might raise relevant questions to sort out confusion, or perhaps suggest that more information be included to help illuminate the themes. Having more involvement from this first line editor is all for the good because she is presumably fluent with the subject. In the next stage, after rewrites are made and queries are answered, the manuscript should go to a copy editor. (Note: If your manuscript is not sent to a copy editor, inquire why not. Not a single word should be released without the copy editor's seal of approval.)

The copy editor is more than a mechanic, responsible for tuning under the hood: He is the guardian of the written word. New writers cannot function without them; old writers have learned to rely on them.

Armed with blue pencils, copy editors will cut through tangled phrases and clauses, and insert em dashes, semicolons, and colons where appropriate. Some will rewrite your garbles, others will make suggestions, and still others will ask you what you meant to say. Sometimes, making a manuscript make sense is as simple as finding better words; other times it demands restructuring many paragraphs—even an entire essay. A good editor is to be listened to, although there is always room for argument. When I said my "In the beginning" phrase was meant to be a cliché, with a wink and a nod to

the reader, my editor understood, tried to make it a little better, yet decided to keep it in. After all, it is my book.

But more often, a skilled copy editor will hear discordant and see misplaced words that are right in front of the writer's eyes yet invisible to him. The writer, even of a technical tract or business exchange, is invested in the writing. The copy editor is not. Sure, he wants the text to be as good as it can be, but in an objective, more or less detached way.

A great copy editor is able to do invasive surgery without leaving a scar. He will remove extraneous this and superfluous that, making the flow of the prose smoother and more enjoyable. If you never compare your original manuscript to the copy-edited version, you will barely know the difference. Reading the "playback" (which is what edited copy is sometimes called), you cannot help but be self-satisfied; you will doubtless say to yourself, "I'm a darn good writer, after all." In fact, the nuanced work was accomplished by the copy editor—who almost never gets credit.

One last thing about the copy editor's role: Reading so many manuscripts requires that the copy editor fact-check. While this job should not be left entirely to the copy editor, it is good to know that someone is watching your back.

(Note: *See Section Three to read "What an Editor Does."*)

Avoiding Clichés

When there is a gap between one's real and one's declared aims, one turns as it were instinctively to long words and exhausted idioms, like cuttlefish squirting out ink. —GEORGE ORWELL

It is embarrassing the way that designers prostrate themselves—and the English language—especially in their promotional material, describing in florid words what they do as though their designs alone aren't enough to tell the story. It may be true that some clients (or prospective clients) don't have a good grasp of what design is, but most have eyes and can intuit. During the nascent period of graphic design (somewhere around the mid-1920s), all that a commercial artist advertising in one of the many promotional annuals had to say was, "Jeanne Doe, calligraphy, layout, illustration," and the point was made (in part because the services were being bought by agencies or art directors, not directly by clients). Today, with nondesign clients being more active in the hiring process, something called "design philosophy" has become the basis of a new patois. Philosophy is not pejorative. But when it turns to sophistry, beware!

For at least the past decade, designers have tried to position themselves as legitimate professionals. Inherent in this quest is an attempt to squelch the myth that visual people are ostensibly illiterate. Where the myth started is anyone's guess. After all, the first, what one might call literate, people—those who developed the earliest codified languages—were image makers. The first alphabets were composed of images. Early scripture was illuminated by scribes who made pictures as well as words—the first typefaces were designed by artists. The first books were designed by artist/writers. So, traditionally, designers have been a very literate people. Then, where and when did the distinction begin? Maybe it came with the onset of commercial printing, when publicity was churned out, not designed—when its makers began to provide a service, not art. Not all commercial printers or commercial artists were enemies of the word, yet the impact of those who were has had a detrimental effect, ultimately leading in the early twentieth century to the schism between copywriters and designers.

During the 1950s these distinctions in the advertising world started to blur, but graphic designers were still suffering from the effects of negative stereotypes. Ever since graphic designers began adding terms such as *marketing* and *communications* to their billheads, the accepted notion that having a codified philosophy would undo those negative stereotypes has resulted in design firms issuing promotional materials replete with weighty (and sometimes dramatic) mission statements that read like either legal briefs or epic poems, like this one:

....
Communications: Visual plays leading to emotional involvement.
Communications: Creativity at levels that make the experience.
Communications: Materials that desire to be collected for keeps.
Communications: Turn the target. Flip the crowd.
Communications: Translate the message into action to your advantage.
Communications: Manage the trains of thought and the rest will come to you for yours.
....

Without any disrespect intended, is what you just read substance or hype? Did it describe or confuse? Think about the selling (flap or ad) copy on a book or the liner notes on a record. In both cases the best of these titillate, if not illuminate. What does this copy tell us? Visual plays? It is a rather strained metaphor. Emotional involvement? It is a lot to hope for from a piece of paper. Collected for keeps? Hold on! Even the best publicity has a limited shelf life. Manage the trains of thought? Hey, did anyone copy-read this?

....
If language be not in accordance with the truth of things, affairs cannot be carried on to success. —CONFUCIUS
....

As hyperbolic as it is, the "visual plays" copy is at least somewhat creative compared with the conventional fare. Indeed, with few welcome exceptions when designers, especially firms, extol their own virtues, the results are dry, platitudinous, and repetitive, with buzzwords reminiscent of police accounts like the ones one hears uttered on the TV news by rookie cops: "The perp, a Caucasian female, was apprehended and subdued by two pursuing, uniformed officers, while proceeding to gain unlawful access to the abode of the victim…."

....
To a teacher of languages there comes a time when the world is but a place of many words and man appears a mere talking animal not more wonderful than a parrot. —JOSEPH CONRAD
....

Like cadets parroting the phrases in Jargon 101 at any police academy, most designers learn—Lord knows from where—that to gain respect in the outside world it is imperative to use officious language they would never apply in everyday

1 HAPPINESS IS A WARM CLIENT

- The process begins with analysis, immersion into the client's situation in order to define the true problem.
- Our primary concern is with our client's success in their business.
- The basic need of most clients who come to us is to fulfill a business function.
- Our primary concern is to solve the client's communications objective.
- Our goal is to meet our client's visual communications needs by applying an approach based on discipline, appropriateness and ambiguity. [Huh?]
- We carefully analyze our client's needs, and if necessary, reinterpret them in a more profound way than the client can do.

- A key element to our approach is that we uniquely tailor each project to a particular client's needs.
- We will not begin a project without a clear understanding of the spoken and unspoken client needs.
- Today, we bring to our clients a rich, ever-expanding base of knowledge and experience.
- Our main concern is understanding and working closely with our clients to carefully think through and define the problem at hand.
- No matter how well we prepare ourselves with information, the client's knowledge far exceeds ours.

3 MEANINGFUL RELATIONSHIPS

- Our professional ability has been developed and tested for 20 years in a highly competitive environment and has been the basis of many enduring relationships.
- We pay special attention to creating strong working relationships among members of the project team. That our approach works has been proven by the unusual amount of repeat business our clients have offered us.
- Recognizing that team effort is required to create successful design, we define our role as a collaborative one.
- We thrive on long-term client relationships, having many major corporate clients for years.
- We nurture the client from beginning to end.

4 DIVERSIFIED MEANINGFUL RELATIONSHIPS

- We've maintained variety in the types of projects and clients that we handle; this has given us the opportunity to develop a diversified portfolio of work.
- Because of our diversity we've attracted a wonderful group of multitalented designers, and we are very proud of them.

2 STYLE? WE DON'T HAVE NO STINKIN' STYLE

- Our approach to design has always been concept-oriented. We feel that a good concept is the single most important aspect of any project. Along with effective design and attention to detail, a strong concept has always made the difference between a good solution and a great one.
- The diversity of our work provides us with the experience and ability to approach a range of design problems in a fresh way.
- Design is the solution of problems, incorporating ideas in relation to the given problem, rather than the arbitrary application of fashionable styles.

- We produce design that goes against the jarring nature of our times.
- We're interested in producing contemporary design, design that's straightforward looking and appropriate for each client.
- Our belief is that any one visual problem has an infinite number of solutions.
- We don't have a style or philosophical framework. We simply want to understand, then solve the problem.
- We do not have a house style, but favor designs which are crisp and simple enough to stand out among today's cluttered communications.

5 TOUCHY-FEELY-SQUEEZY

- Graphic design should touch the viewer as well as inform.
- Imagination and sensibility create the most potent visual communication.
- It's not that we don't believe in a structure or grid; we just believe they should be felt instead of seen.
- We try to balance our own personal insight with the client's particular needs—design is a magical balance.

6 THE FIRST DAY OF THE REST OF OUR LIVES

- Every client, project and problem is unpredictable. Each is unique. Our mission as a group is to solve the unique problem, manage the unusual project, and serve our wary client the best quality design available.
- We welcome the challenge of different business involvements.
- Our experience allows us to approach a range of design problems in a fresh way.

7 HOW DO I LOVE ME?

- We take great pride in a body of work that has received national recognition for excellence and in the roster of prestigious clients who hired us to create it.

usage. No school, however, exists to teach this stuff—yet take virtually any promotional brochure for a design firm, scratch the surface, and you will find variations of the following platitudes:

- Design is a tool for achieving specific results. Being responsive, we begin each project by learning exactly what results our client expects. This then becomes our communications goal.
- Establishing an appropriate, positive emphasis is the key. This, in conjunction with good graphic design, is our special skill.
- Our work exhibits a great diversity of styles and imagery. In an era of design specialists, we invariably believe that as varied as the messages are, so should the means of conveying them.

These statements by three very different design firms are not inherently disingenuous, but when viewed as representative of most promo copy, they are formulaic. Should all selling copy sound alike? Imagine what the prospective client who gets pitched by many designers must think after reading the same phrases and sentiments over and over. The client probably thinks they've all read the same copy of *How to Succeed in Business without Really Trying*, or at least have hired the same PR firm.

To further the point that, despite the remarkable diversity among design firms today—their hype comes from the same copy of Bartlett's *Familiar Design Firm Promotions*—the following phrases have been culled from a variety of sources. In fact, virtually no two of the design firms represented by these unattributed statements do the same kind of work. For purposes of clarity they are organized according to the six major thematic categories.

One has to wonder whether these designers and firms read one another's promotional material or whether these pearls just develop over time in their own hermetically sealed environments. Design firms tend to stink of their own perfume. In fact, virtually all of the designers represented by the statements on the previous pages are fluid and literate when talking about their work. But put them in front of a keyboard and they choke up.

Of course, there are those who eschew the conventions of promo writing. Some designers have gone overboard in the other direction, emphasizing human, rather than business, values, such as this one: "During our day, we encourage pride but not possessiveness." Rarely, in an open-office environment can an idea emerge and evolve without being "touched" by more than one person. This interaction is what tests the idea to ensure its rightfulness. Others prefer wit and humor, such as this send-up of a famous quote: "When I hear the words design philosophy I reach for my X-Acto." (The reference being to Hermann Göring, who said, "When I hear the word culture, I reach for my Browning!")

But the most understated and curiously poetic piece that this writer ever read can be attributed to Henry Wolf in the book *New York Design*: "My firm is not unique but it combines the facilities of photography and design under one roof. I photograph for my own concepts." Though this quote is a masterpiece of clarity and concision, one might nevertheless wonder, does he get much work?

The Music of Words

When I was a graphic designer, I orchestrated words into a symphony of typefaces. They were not my words, so I typographically interpreted other people's thoughts and meanings. They weren't my typefaces either; I simply selected and composed them to make a demonstrative expression of content. When writing, however, the orchestration of the manuscript goes hand in glove with the composition of the prose. Writing is as much about achieving harmony or tension between words in a sentence as it is about conveying the facts.

Experienced writers have a rather deep reservoir of words. Less experienced ones may rely on tried-and-true words and phrases. They may also jump headfirst into the thesaurus or synonym finder to seek good alternatives. Using these tools is not cheating, although it is often not as effective as you would think. While some synonyms fit nicely into the sentence, many are not custom made for what is written. The wrong-sounding word, even if it has the correct meaning, stands out as strained.

Writing about design is not poetry, per se. But there is no reason not to be poetic when appropriate—or at least interesting. The ultimate bugaboo of any writing is the b-word:

"All good design is storytelling. All good storytelling is design."

boring. Just as meandering, idle patter at a cocktail party is uninspiring, the stringing together of words, no matter how clear the meaning is, will induce a yawn. Words have rhythm, bravado, and drama when used in the right combinations and proper syntax. Why must a business report be dry? Why should an academic paper lack character? Often, just a well-placed word or simple phrase can turn the commonplace into a vibrant crescendo.

Telling Stories

I tell my design students: "All good design is storytelling." I tell my writing students: "All good storytelling is design." Storytelling is the new buzz-mantra, and the s-word has been overused lately. Perhaps reality TV and real-time online videos bring out the storyteller in all of us. It appears that everyone wants to tell stories. So, all art, design, science, and technology are rooted in storytelling more than ever before. What are the renowned TED conferences but storytelling mash-ups? Erstwhile amateurs use the term *narrative arc* in as common-place a manner as *font* (once only used by professionals).

Nonetheless, storytelling and narrative are essential to the design writing process. Without story—or plot, if you will—what have you got? Even a factual business report can tell a tale, albeit often in a neutral manner. Not all stories have to be dramatic or melodramatic. Storytelling is simply the expression of something you, as the writer, believe is of interest to you, as the reader. Indeed, you may well be representative of your average reader.

I was writing an article recently about a graphic designer who accomplished something I thought would be a terrific story to share with my audience (including you). The entire piece is reproduced here. But I will also highlight certain parts that make this a story worth telling, rather than a mere report. Here's my story:

Paula Scher, a respected designer and good friend, insisted that I meet Johnny Selman, who recently received his graduate

degree in design and was a newcomer to New York. Not knowing what to expect, other than Scher having given him a two-thumbs-up recommendation, he pulled out a thick volume filled with reproductions of posters he had made. At first glance, they were handsome though reminiscent of other designers I knew. Then he told me there were 365 posters designed over the course of a year—one a day—based on news reports from the BBC. He religiously produced a highly sophisticated, conceptually astute visual diary, which was posted daily on a website and then collected in the volume before me. I knew immediately that I wanted to tell his story.

Like the posters, I wanted to make it a story that could be easily digested and appreciated—no more, no less. I also wanted to make it less ephemeral than it was. Since he completed his project in 2011, it was already many months old. I wanted the reader to feel his excitement and understand his process, while not having to consider whether or not it was "breaking news." My method was to give it a timeless, rather than timely, lead:

....

Ever wonder what a graphic designer does to wile away the idle hours? Johnny Selman spends every morning ritually checking headlines on the BBC. But that's not all. In 2010, "I decided to create a poster a day for twenty days in reaction to a headline for each day," he recently told me.

....

The first sentence establishes the idea that this is not just a story about a former student's thesis, but rather a self-initiated challenge. Selman's work is the protagonist, so the authorial voice was there to move things along, connect the dots, and provide context. An edited interview with Selman provided the true voice and the firsthand details. I was particularly glad he provided his checklist. While not exciting prose, in an instant it gives the reader a sense of Selman's criteria (see page 42). But first, our case study:

CASE STUDY:

POSTER-A-DAY: A VISUAL VITAMIN

STEVEN HELLER

Originally published February 24, 2012 on *The Daily Heller*, http://imprint.printmag.com/daily-heller

Ever wonder what a graphic designer does to wile away the idle hours[?] Johnny Selman spends every morning ritually checking headlines on the BBC. But that's not all. In 2010, "I decided to create a poster a day for 20 days in reaction to a headline for each day," he recently told me. This exercise triggered the idea for his Academy of Art University in San Francisco graduate school thesis, which he expanded into 365 days of posters and world news he calls BBCx365. It is a tour de force.

"The purpose of this project is to promote the awareness of global current events with the American public," he wrote in an introduction to his website. "'American citizens know little about current events in general and even less about overseas events,' according to the *Washington Post* in 2006."

The changing pool of content kept the project exciting, he says. "I created a tight set of design parameters to ensure that the project would hang together as a set at the end of the day. I reduced the composition to its simplest visual form and removed all unnecessary elements from the designs. The most challenging aspect to the project, outside the Groundhog Day–like repetition, was the importance of creating designs based on rich ideas."

Slow news days are inevitable, but Selman tried to instill a sense of urgency and importance to every story he represented in the hopes that someone would be inspired by even the more monotonous of news days. Still, keeping up the pace day after day, approaching every story as new and maintaining a

semblance [of] originality, had to be a chore. "I had elements of gestural drawing in my posters," he explains, "and many times I would reuse bits and pieces of an already used image to provoke a different thought. There were times when using a repetitive image added to the poster's meaning, such as the two posters about the Dutch family that was held captive by pirates in Somalia. The reuse of the imagery helped bring closure to an already told story."

Rigor is imperative when creating a daily poster. So Selman's list of dos and don'ts included [the following]: "Use as few elements as possible. Reduce the story to its simplest visual form. Don't overthink it. Don't overwork it. Use as few colors as possible. Use flat color. Use color as a representative element. Don't use gradients. Use typography as the central visual element whenever possible. Use Gotham Bold or your hand. When needed use Tungsten Bold as a condensed face. Other typefaces can be used sparingly for parody. Use bitmap and vector graphics. Rip the levels out of photographs. Keep it interesting. Use humor. Use parody. Use satire. Use visual puns. Stay neutral. Be bold. Don't be afraid."

The task he set for himself was challenging at best, and exhausting too. Some days he just wanted to sleep in. "In order to maintain sanity within a task like this you have to allow yourself room to breathe and give yourself a break once in a while," he notes. "It was best to start my posters when I was feeling inspired or up to the task. It made the process go quicker than if I forced myself to sit and stare at my computer or endlessly sketch in my notebook."

But [Selman says] the project became "the constant in my life." Through sickness, vacation, injury, work, and even a houseboat bachelor party, the daily design ritual was there like a backbone. "A deadline that was as predictable as the temperature in San Francisco."

The posters vary in conceptual acuity, but on the whole Selman's visual shorthand is up to the task. There are also traces of various other poster designers, including [Josef Müller-] Brockmann, Armin Hofmann, James Victore, and others who view economy as a virtue.

Selman insists the marathon had an ultimate purpose: to take complex information and to distill it down into digestible bites. "I certainly learned about time management," he adds. "I learned how to deal with the barrage of anonymous online criticism [the series had an online component that drew many yeas and nays]."

In the final analysis, Selman, who graduated in December 2011, admits "the skill set I gained during the course of the project can be directly applied to many aspects of visual communication. I'm working in New York now and am involved in some really exciting projects. Most of all, I'm making up for lost time with my wife. We are quickly referring to events in our lives as pre- or post-posters."

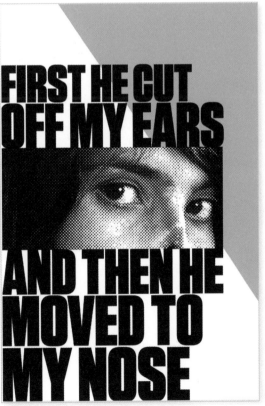

Quite a year for news. Here Selman covers Allahu Akbar, a suicide bomber, and the female victim of Islamic fundamentalist law in Afghanistan who was mutilated based on a religious decree.

Johnny Selman, designed a poster a day for a year based
on headline stories on the BBC news report. Included
are the Egyptian revolt against President Hosni
Mubarak; Rocket attacks from Gaza into
Israel; the trial against hate crime defendants.

Rigor is imperative when creating a daily poster. So Selman's list of dos and don'ts included: "Use as few elements as possible. Reduce the story to its simplest visual form. Don't overthink it. Don't over-work it. Use as few colors as possible. Use flat color. Use color as a representative element. Don't use gradients. Use typography as the central visual element whenever possible. Use Gotham Bold or your hand. When needed use Tungsten Bold as a condensed face. Other typefaces can be used sparingly for parody. Use bitmap and vector graphics. Rip the levels out of photographs. Keep it interesting. Use humor. Use parody. Use satire. Use visual puns. Stay neutral. Be bold. Don't be afraid."

This is not a dramatic story. There are no highs and lows, twists and turns, or Earth-shaking surprises. It is about a process that may be instructive, inspiring, or both. So to make it a story worth reading, I bolstered Selman's voice through small narrative bridges. Here's one:

The task he set for himself was challenging at best, and exhausting too. Some days he just wanted to sleep in.

Everyone can relate to "wanting to sleep in." Here is another bridge that includes his candid description:

But the project became "the constant in my life." Through sickness, vacation, injury, work, and even a houseboat bachelor party, the daily design ritual was there like a backbone. "A deadline that was as predictable as the temperature in San Francisco."

Storytelling is taking the commonplace and making it special. Notice I did not say "transformative" or "transcendent" (two of my favorite hyperboles). Stories do not have to rise to the biblical level. A good story, like good design, must simply provide the service it was created for. You write for a purpose, if only to share ideas worth sharing. So when you are writing an essay, [an] article, and even a report or proposal, you can effectively convey the story you want to tell (of course, make certain you have a story to tell); then the mechanics of good writing can function as they are meant to.

Pitching a Story

There are many ways to pitch, suggest, or sell a story, essay, or book idea to an editor. If you have authorial credibility already it is easier than if you are a first-time writer. Yet for both, it is useful to make clips and writing samples available so that an editor can review your craft. Writing is a meritocracy. The fact is that all editors, in whichever media you can name, want to identify (and often discover) good writers. The more profes-sionally trained the better. But even if you are untrained, the high quality of your writing will often seal the deal.

Editors swoon over good ideas. While they frequently assign an idea to writers, they are just as happy—maybe more so—to have them served up fresh on a platter. Conversely, they dislike stale or undercooked ideas. Make certain your idea is original and you can fulfill your promise to make it scintillating. In pitching an idea you do not need the entire concept written out, but the fundamental content should be vividly sketched and outlined. This will prove that you have confidence in your own notion.

The best way to accomplish a successful pitch is to write a short paragraph or précis that explains the idea in a couple of sentences. This is known as an "elevator pitch." Then add the means or method you will probably use to achieve your goal. Your pitch should be smartly written, but need not be too formal. Confidence is your best ally. Just be concise and interesting. Make the editor hungry for the final course—the actual text—by feeding just a taste of the story's most salient parts.

A book idea should be pitched in much the same way. But since a book is a larger investment for an editor and publisher, much more content is required (everything from an outline to a full-blown dummy). Even then it may go through a few revisions before an offer to publish is made. Rockport editor, Emily Potts, wrote the following essay as a guide to getting published.

CASE STUDY:
PUBLISHING YOUR BOOK
Getting the Green Light

EMILY POTTS

Emily Potts is senior acquisitions editor at Rockport Publishers
(Originally published December 16, 2011 on Felt & Wire, *www.feltandwire.com/2011/12/16/publishing-your-book-getting-greenlighted/)*

So you think you have a great book idea? A lot of people do, but if you don't have a solid proposal, your book will never see the light of day. Publishers have strict guidelines for book briefs for a reason: Producing a book requires a huge up-front investment, and it's a gamble.

As acquisitions editor for Rockport Publishers, I'm the first point of contact for aspiring authors. If you can't sell the idea to me, that's as far as it goes. If I think your concept has merit, I will work with you to develop a book brief and be your biggest champion in the process. Just because a book idea has a strong concept, however, doesn't mean it will be published. There are many factors involved in the approval process, and ultimately the decision to publish the book will be made by an in-house committee [composed] of marketing and sales people. If they don't understand it or don't think they can sell it, it's dead.

Here are the dos and don'ts of submitting a book proposal:

- **Don't submit a finished manuscript.** Editors don't have time to review an entire manuscript, nor do they want to. Send a summary of your book. This can include a table of contents and a sample chapter. It allows the editor to see how you organized your content, and she can review your writing abilities. Your cover letter should explain the book concept —but be succinct.

- **Know the publisher and what they publish.** I can't tell you how many times I've received proposals from people on topics ranging from foot massage to tractor maintenance. In most cases, the author is doing a mass mailing to any and all publishers, which is costly and a waste of time—your letter will end up in the trash. Research publishers and target the ones that publish books in the category you're pitching.

- **Know your target audience.** Publishers are in the business of selling books, so give specific information on who will buy your book and why. Will readers need it to help them excel on the job? Will educators want to pick it up for required reading in their courses? If you can get statistics that prove this book is needed, do it.

- **Tell why your audience will plunk down cold, hard cash.** With so much information available online, you need to provide a convincing argument why people will make an investment in your book. What's different about it from what's already out there? Be specific here.

Just because a book idea has a strong concept, however, doesn't mean it will be published. There are many factors involved in the approval process, and ultimately the decision to publish the book will be made by an in-house committee...

- **Know the competition. Research books on the same subject/category—what will your book bring to the market that's different?** How successful are the other books? Amazon.com provides book ranking numbers as well as the categories they fall in, and this makes it easy to find similar books. It usually works in your favor if these books are selling well, because that suggests they're in a category of interest to lots of people. Note the titles, prices, page counts, and when they were published, and then point out what these titles offer compared to what your book will offer.

- **Explain why you are the best person to write/deliver this material.** Show your qualifications and experiences as they relate to the topic you're writing about.

- **Offer ideas on how you'll promote the book. Once the book is finished, there's still a lot of work to be done.** Publishers expect authors—especially well-known authors—to promote the book and reach out to prospective readers. Social media come in handy here. Do you have an online following either on a blog or [on] Twitter? Will you write articles and do interviews prior to publication? If so, what contacts do you have? Are you a good public speaker? Offer to do a book signing at your local bookstore. Every little bit helps, so be sure to put all the possibilities in your proposal. If the publisher feels confident in your abilities to promote your book to a big enough audience, there's a better chance of it getting approved.

- **Have everything in place with your contacts, and be sure you can meet the editorial deadlines before you sign a contract.** Don't promise the moon if you can't deliver. Meeting deadlines is important. You're not the only person working on your book. There is a team of people at the publishing house who also have deadlines to meet, and they are usually working on many books at one time. Be respectful of their schedules, as time has already been carved out for your book.

Writing a book is a huge commitment for everyone involved, and the process can be painful. But if it's done right, you'll have a product you can be proud of that will hopefully take on a life of its own.

SORT

GATHER

RESEARCH

PROCESS

RESULTS

RESEARCH
Building the Narrative Foundation

Ideas are good. But where do you get them? Some people believe they fly around like radio waves just waiting to be captured by the brain's receiver. Perhaps it is the way some people, those who wear silver foil on their heads, get them. But the majority of us develop ideas from terra firma—or rather quantifiable fact. Even most fiction is built on fact.

That's where research is essential. Research is the process of gathering, sorting, and processing information. You build your writing on the results of your research. The word is often construed in academic terms as a rigorous process of acquisition. In fact, research can be light or heavy depending on the scope of your work. Some research demands deep archaeological digging. Other research requires only a few Google reference searches. This section addresses ways and means of research and how to collect it in such a way that it effectively and efficiently serves your needs.

Database Research

Class dismissed! Now, let's get back to the computer. There is no denying that we have access to the most powerful desktops ever conceived on this planet. The amount of information, knowledge, and even shared wisdom at our fingertips was inconceivable when the first mainframes were spitting out punch cards. But the challenge is how to capture the information you need. What to accept as truth or fancy could easily be Solomonic in scope. So, it is useful to chart out a research strategy.

Great research is partly police work. You find clues that lead to more clues that lead to a hot trail that leads to conclusive evidence. Often you may instinctively "feel" something exists somewhere, but finding it is the result of luck and serendipity. You stumble over a document that leads you to an archive that provides you with a key, and so on. Despite that thrill of discovery, having a plan that takes you from point A to point B is useful.

Your road will start at your computer when you log on to the WorldCat.org (www.worldcat.org), an online resource that compiles, aggregates, and otherwise spits up all the known archives, libraries, collections, and repositories in the world. For scholarly research this database is essential. But it supports nonscholarly research as well. Almost every museum, library, and archive maintains (or will launch) its own database systems. The interconnectivity enabled by the Web, combined with the availability of countless digitized rare and valuable documents, creates intense research potential.

Warning: If you are a research nerd, try to stick with your strategy. It is very easy to get sidetracked and wander off. Make a note of other areas of interest and revisit them after you've done your intended work. I know what I'm talking about, because even as I write this, an amazing gravitational force is pulling me toward an archive on....

Library and Museum Research

Sitting at home in front of the computer is convenient (even cozy) and expedient, but not altogether useful for hands-on research. You can read. You can see. But you cannot touch, feel, or smell. When writing about design—even digital or virtual design—you want to hold the object. You must physically experience, in whatever way you can, its manufacture, tactility, and functionality to determine whether it meets its goal or your expectation. The comfort, or lack thereof, in a beautifully ornamented chair can only be tested in person. A beautifully typeset printed book may be flawed because of the paper it uses. This cannot be determined on-screen.

Libraries and museums (and museum libraries) offer an opportunity to lay your hands on a variety of materials. If some are so fragile that firsthand contact is prohibited, at the very least you can view the original materials from a safe distance.

Visiting the library, talking with the librarian, and skimming through the card or online catalogue may be time-consuming, but it is often time well spent.

Primary Resources

Primary resources are those rarities you uncover for yourself. They are the seminal documents; the original work; the forgotten copy. Whatever has not already been prodded, investigated, and analyzed by someone else, is primary.

A primary resource can be a personal library or archive, corporate repository, or library and museum holdings—and let's not forget the firsthand interview. Some are catalogued, others are not. By way of example, there are three significant archives that specifically focus on graphic design research: The Milton Glaser Design Study Center and Archives, a

division of the Visual Arts Foundation, is "dedicated to preserving and making accessible design works of significant artistic, cultural, and historical value by preeminent designers, illustrators, and art directors who have close ties to the School of Visual Arts. The collections represent the artistic and intellectual vitality of the SVA community, and provide an invaluable resource to students, designers, and researchers who wish to study the breadth of a designer's work."

The Archives acquires materials in many formats with the intent to document the design process from conception to completion. Among the media held by the Archives are posters, works of art on paper, printed samples and ephemera, photographs, audio tapes and videotapes, publications, scrapbooks, slides, and personal papers.

The Herb Lubalin Study Center of Design and Typography in the School of Art was founded in 1985 by The Cooper Union and friends of the late Herb Lubalin. According to its website, "Its mission is to focus on the preservation of design history through its core collection of the work of Herb Lubalin and extensive library and archive of design ephemera. The Study Center and its archive are important central resources for the students and faculty as well as the professional and general public. All materials are fully available by appointment and are regularly highlighted through the center's public exhibitions and lecture programming."

The Graphic Design Archives at Rochester Institute of Technology, founded in 1984, documents and preserves the work of significant American graphic designers active from the 1920s to the 1950s, as well as selected contemporary designers working in the modernist traditions, including Walter Allner, Hans J. Barschel, Saul Bass, Lester Beall, Alexey Brodovitch, Will Burtin, Tom Carnase, Chermayeff & Geismar, Louis Danziger, Estelle Ellis, Mary Faulconer, George Giusti, William Golden, Rob Roy Kelly, Leo Lionni, Alvin Lustig, Joyce Morrow, Cipe Pineles, Paul Rand, Alex Steinweiss, Ladislav Sutnar, Ceil Smith Thayer, Bradbury Thompson, Fred Troller, and Massimo and Lella Vignelli. The collections contain original source materials documenting the designers' working lives, and include such unique items as original artwork, sketchbooks, sculptures, architectural

Q/A Beth Kleber Talks about Research

Beth Kleber is the archivist at Milton Glaser Design Study Center and Archives, School of Visual Arts, New York.

In researching design materials, what is the most valuable resource?

As an archivist, I'm generally most interested in tracking down materials that reside in archives. The best place to start this kind of research is WorldCat.org, a collaborative library catalog that allows you to search the holdings of thousands of libraries. It is best used as a jumping-off point, a place to begin with a generalized search based on a designer or client or subject area, which can lead to more item-specific information in a library catalog or archival finding aid.

As a researcher what tool or tip do you have for organizing and retaining information?

My background as an archivist and librarian seems to permeate all aspects of my life; I categorize obsessively. When I'm doing online research, I make generous use of Delicious bookmarks (http://delicious.com), using the same subject and material tags that I use in my work.

What are the advantages and disadvantages of researching in an archive?

Archival research has some built-in difficulties. Archives can be a bit daunting to the uninitiated: They require an advance appointment and (often) the researcher's ability to specify exactly what they're interested in seeing; they are not designed for browsing. Archives' holdings are described in detailed text inventories called "finding aids," which can be tricky to interpret, especially when you're dealing with visual materials. The upside is, obviously, access to original materials and a window into the designer's process, thanks to sketches, original art, and any other supporting materials. Archives adhere to the organizational principle of original order, so the opportunity to see materials in the order in which the creator arranged them can reveal something about how that person viewed their own work. Finally, archives provide the tantalizing possibility of uncovering something that is unpublished and as-yet-unseen by the general public.

↑ **Posters by Heinz Edelman** at the Milton Glaser Design Study Center and Archives.

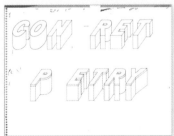

Poster and sketch by Milton Glaser for the School of Visual Arts, New York

models, reliefs, and printed samples (tear sheets, proofs, and sample issues of publications).

Many other archives that include graphic design, such as The Wolfsonian Museum and Archives of American Art, can be identified and located through WorldCat.org. As a rule, if you do not have more personal access materials, these resources will provide the more intimate experience that defines primary research.

Secondary Resources

Secondary research includes existing texts, exhibitions, documentaries, collections, and so on, that have already been vetted by other researchers. Incorporating existing research into your own is an accepted practice as long as credit is given where it is due. Quoting, paraphrasing, and otherwise "borrowing" another's work should be handled with care but used diligently when appropriate.

The resources are fairly obvious: books, magazines, newspapers, catalogues, brochures, and more. There is, however, a fine line between secondary and primary when it comes to certain of the above. The rarity of a document could mean it is indeed an original source. Most articles published in graphic design journals from, say, 100 years ago, are probably as seminal as you can get. Still, they must be cited appropriately and described accurately. For secondary graphic design research, never underestimate what has already been produced. Trade magazines abound with firsthand accounts of designers'

own work. Arguably the best resources for printed material with credits and a modicum of analysis are the design annuals based on annual competitions, including (ones still in print) *Communication Arts*, *Print* magazine's Regional Issue, *HOW* magazine, *The Art Directors Club*, and *The Type Directors Club*, among others. The AIGA maintains the AIGA Design Archives online. It claims on its website that it is "one of the richest online resources available to those who practice, study and appreciate great design."

The AIGA Design Archives includes more than 20,000 selections from the AIGA's annual juried design competitions dating from 1924 through the present. In addition, it features special collections of major American design firms and practitioners whose design accomplishments might otherwise not be preserved online or made available to the public. These now include the work of Chermayeff & Geismar (1960–2006), Vignelli Associates (1962–2008), and Push Pin Graphic (1960–2005). For a firsthand experience, some of the physical artifacts in the collections are available for research and study at the AIGA Archives at the Denver Art Museum in Colorado and the Rare Book and Manuscript Library at Columbia University's Butler Library in New York.

With these and the additional worldwide resources made accessible through WorldCat.org, the globe is made ever smaller for the primary and secondary researcher.

Q/A Alexander Tochilovsky Talks about Archives

Alexander Tochilovsky is the curator at the Herb Lubalin Study Center of Design and Typography, School of Art, The Cooper Union, New York.

Where do you find the most relevant information on design objects?

I am finding more and more that design periodicals offer a tremendous amount of information for design research, especially the more obscure titles prevalent in the design and advertising trade during the 1960s. Other, more established, magazines also offer a lot of information. The challenge is typically the fact that few are indexed fully, or even partially. So it involves a lot of poring over the issues in hopes of finding leads. Accessing library records often helps to narrow the search a bit. In that sense, libraries still offer the most

valuable entry point for a lot of material. Thankfully, there are a lot of resources and catalogs available online, so finding a library which may have a specific copy of a magazine has become much easier. Another valuable resource for me is the fact that the Internet has become so much more visually oriented. So much so that often I am able to find pieces or at least leads by simply doing a web search. Sometimes sellers on eBay or Etsy will list the table of contents of a particular issue of a magazine, and all of a sudden a previously hidden bit of information will become uncovered. I have had countless instances like that in the past few years of research.

What is your surefire tip for retaining and organizing information?

I tend to rely on old-fashioned but trusted methods of photocopies, note pads, tape recorder, and a pen. I remember and retain a lot on my own, so the tools simply help me to have quicker access to the specifics. Diligence in noting sources of information helps in the long run. I have also started using outlining tools and applications to keep track of images, leads, and other information that comes mainly from the Web. One of the applications that seem to be the best fit for the way I tend to work is called Evernote. It's still not the dominant form of organization for me, but it helps quite a bit. I like that it is accessible across devices and I can get to the information remotely if needed.

What is the value of archives?

The advantages of researching in an archive are that you are afforded a breadth of materials to explore. The best part is that there is a better sense of the context behind the work, as there is usually more than just the work itself. Letters, manuscripts, correspondences, slides, notes, etc., all add to a fuller picture behind the ephemera. The other advantage is that you are typically dealing with knowledgeable staff who are familiar with the contents and can better direct you. Within an archive you also get to see the whole range of someone's work. It is an unedited perspective on an individual's or a studio's output. You can observe the evolution of the work, of an aesthetic including things that in some cases may be duds, or on the other hand great work that had been rejected by a client. The disadvantages are that you typically are confronted with an intimidating amount of material to sort through. It can be somewhat overwhelming, especially when so much of the research is reliant on looking at the actual material. Even if there are finding aids, it's still necessary to look at and handle the work—which may not be such a bad thing after all.

↑ **Wall of logos** designed by Herb Lubalin

↑ **Samples of work** by Herb Lubalin

↑ **Library** at the Herb Lubalin Study Center

NO GOOGLE!
Research without the Web

Google is the best research tool since the invention of card catalogs. Nonetheless, I teach a class called "No Google" at the School of Visual Arts, New York. It may seem unnecessarily cruel to withhold such a fundamental tool, but watching students squirm is only a small part of the fun.

Internet search engines cannot solve all research challenges. So the purpose of this class is to teach gumshoe rather than desktop research. My goal is to encourage research projects based on personal or scholarly interests, historical artifacts, or found objects. Analysis rooted in firsthand interplay is essential.

Design objects are found through various archives, libraries, antiques markets, attics, and countless other venues. Design objects can be broadly defined as being in two or three dimensions and having the properties of being professionally conceived with a particular purpose and function. They can also be vernacular objects, not necessarily designed by professionals yet having a decidedly specific purpose or function. Art for art's sake should, however, be avoided unless a case can be made for functionality. Each object—new or old—becomes the basis for a research narrative, a story of origins, applications, and consequences.

There are two assignments: the warm-up and the primary project. The warm-up (three weeks) is a scavenger hunt. Here's what I tell the students:

"For this project you are required to visit any of the flea markets or antiques stores in New York City to locate a piece of design (preferably unique—i.e., no clichéd wood type, please) that will serve as the basis for a short story. Once identified, this object will become the core or starting point for a disquisition on its significance in relation to its genre and/or the context in which it was created."

↑ **Lorraine Hair nets**, which started Chappell Ellisson on her research.

The outcome is a five-minute "slide" presentation presented before the class. Sounds simple enough, but the presentation must be a finely honed narrative that reveals something about the object that gives it gravitas or larger meaning.

One student, Chappell Ellison, followed the trail of a 1940s woman's bouffant hair net. The basic product history was interesting enough, but what developed as she delved into the microfilm revealed that one Harry Glemby, the wealthy manufacturer/designer, had been the victim of a major jewel robbery. Okay, his misfortune had nothing to do with the design of the net, but a strong dramatic narrative was built around it.

Another student, Derrick Mead, developed a story about a box of blasting caps (circa 1900), which he found in an old

Las Venus
+
Paul Smith

Thanks,
Laura!

←**Sarah Froelich's** visual research diary.

barn. While the box design piqued his interest, his research ultimately turned into a history about the evolution of not just the box, but of the cap design and the role it played in American agriculture and industry.

The longer project I call "Design as Protagonist" demands more scholarly rigor, while maintaining an eye and ear for "story." Here is the charge:

"You are required to focus on one or more objects from any research resource. It can be either functional or ornamental design—large or small, current or vintage. You must report on the history of the object, including its manufacture, design, application, development, influence, and any other relevant details. This should develop into a bigger narrative."

In this project the object is a window onto other narrative threads. Look hard enough and invariably something materializes. Over the course of the semester the students report on their progress in uncovering, recording, and analyzing the object and its affinities. The final presentation is a 2,000–3,000-word document and a 10-minute oral presentation.

One student, Sarah Froelich, became so obsessed with tracking down the designers of Dansk cooking pots—notably one used for paella—that she traveled to Denmark several times to meet with pot designers and their families. Another student,

Anna Kealey, fascinated by the typography used on the album cover for a dramatic reading of the bestselling sixties sexploitation book *The Sensuous Woman*, exhaustively tracked down many of the creators of the book and record. While she didn't learn much about the type, she discovered why it was produced as a sound recording from the actual participants.

Since design objects do not exist in a vacuum, in addition to exploring the context in which the objects reside, students must evaluate them in terms of effectiveness, consequence, and overall influence on the culture. The results are indeed "object lessons" that serve as building blocks of critical design writing.

Students are not required to adhere to any single research methodology, but are nonetheless required to explain their research process as part of their story—which involves locating resources the old-fashioned way, often by physically collecting their materials.

At no time shall Google or any search engine be used to either locate or research the objects, unless....well, actually, there is a loophole, but the students have to solve that riddle for themselves. Of course, after the class is over, the students can Google to their hearts' content. But I guarantee Google will never replace hands-on involvement or (hint, hint) befriending a truly enthusiastic librarian.

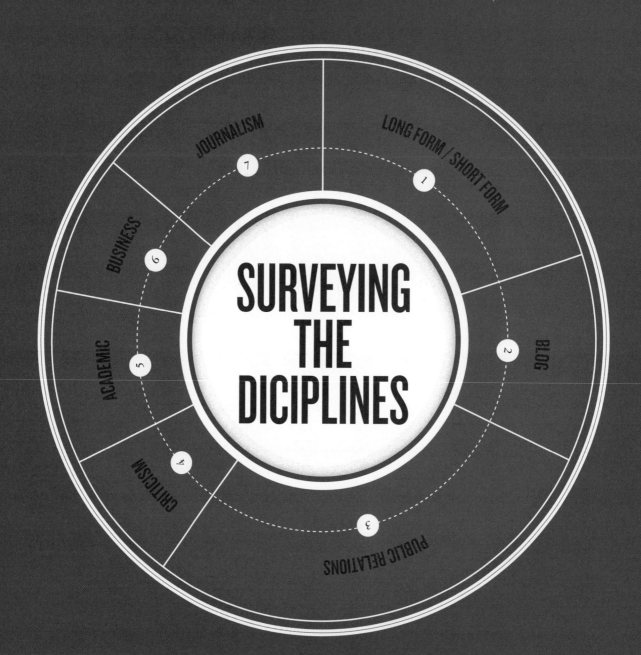

SURVEYING
THE
DICIPLINES

LONG FORM / SHORT FORM 1

BLOG 2

PUBLIC RELATIONS 3

CRITICISM 4

ACADEMIC 5

BUSINESS 6

JOURNALISM 7

You have something to say. You want to write about it. But do you know what discipline, form, or genre you need to perfect? Options abound. What's more, it is not necessary to select just one or two. Of course, being a generalist—knowing many methods—opens considerably more doors than not. Yet mastering your special metier can't hurt. Before you are the opportunities.

Starting clockwise (with the chart on the left) you must know the difference between long and short form; understand what is a blog and how to craft stories for it; what distinguishes public relations from prose writing; where criticism fits into both journalism and academic writing; the difference between writing for your business and writing in general—then there are all the nuances in between. Of course, rules exist for good writing, but intuition plays a role. Do you write in the first or third person? Do you avoid certain words or structures?

By surveying these disciplines they are bound to become clearer. Once you've understood these distinctions, then its time to make your words come to life.

① LONG FORM / SHORT FORM

Do you like to write long or short? Long equals around 1,000 words or more—a long essay, article, scholarly paper, or book. Short is from 250 to 1,000 words—an extended caption to a short essay or column. Skill is needed for both. And it is often harder to write short than long.

An editor will usually dictate how long you must write to fill the space. Some periodicals are predicated on short stories; others include a mix, but maybe never exceeding, say, 2,000 words. Sometimes you will dictate how long you want or need to write. The case studies that follow are of different lengths owing to either editorial or authorial demands. The former must budget space, the latter must respond to the needs of the story. If you have considerable and meaty research, it may be impossible to write short. Conversely, many subjects are better when concise.

For many neophytes it might seem that writing short is a virtue. After all, you do not have to fill up space with descriptions (or as Homer Simpson comically achieves it by writing "Screw Flanders" over and over). Nonetheless, both approaches can be found in the long-form/short-form discipline as well as the other six disciplines covered in this section of the book. As you read each case study in Section Two, keep in mind how economical or expansive is the composition of the writing.

Akiko Busch has been writing both long and short on design and cultural themes for over twenty years. Here she discusses her attraction to the designed world.

Q/A Akiko Busch Talks about Being a Design User

Akiko Busch is the author of The Uncommon Life of Common Objects.

What draws you to a topic?

I come to design as a user, so it's the interaction between the object—or room or building or landscape—and the user that interests me; and how that engages the imagination, or doesn't, for better or for worse.

Why do you feel it is important to examine our relationship to and with objects?

Because it is so incongruous, strange, improbable, and often so illogical, but human beings are also so deeply capable of having emotional relationships with inanimate objects.

What do you look for in an object in order to write about it?

Both its capacity for emotional engagement and its ability to reflect unexpected truths about the world it inhabits.

How do you usually research a piece?

With any luck, from a variety of perspectives: That of the designer; users of different ages and backgrounds; critics; how the object may have been represented in a piece of fiction; referenced in a poem; or appeared in a film; and how the object endures and mutates over time are a few of them.

2 JOURNALISM

Journalism encompasses various methods. Reportage is the accumulation and presentation of facts through eyewitness accounts and commentaries, woven together to reveal an event or phenomenon. While criticism can be journalism, reportage is not necessarily meant to be critical or analytical. Interpretation is left for commentators, who intermingle fact and educated supposition. In the design field much of the writing has been "trade journalism," a method of explaining to professionals what is occurring in their world(s).

In recent years, more critical analysis and personal points of view have been injected into design writing, particularly with an ear and eye toward introducing nondesigners to design concepts. Alice Twemlow, a design writer and chair of the MFA Design Criticism program at the School of Visual Arts, New York, writes often for the mass market. How to get across design issues in a more general journalistic context, and how to discuss the everyday in design terms, has been a matter of great skill. She addresses this in the following case study.

What skills should one actively cultivate for good design writing?

Probably the same skills in most other kinds of writing: attentiveness, unprejudiced inquiry, a bit of skepticism, a sense of history, and—one way or another—arriving at a sense of clarity about what you want to say.

A technical question: How important is your opening sentence, and how do you approach creating it?

Vital—but there is no single formula for finding it. Sometimes the lead presents itself clearly, right up front, but often it does not. It may come a bit later as the story is refined and articulated. Because writing about anything is such an associative process, the progression of the story can easily morph.

When writing a story, do you have the reader in mind?

In a distant and abstract way, perhaps, but the reader does not usually factor into what I am writing about.

CASE STUDY:
DESIGN JOURNALISM FOR THE MASS MARKET

ALICE TWEMLOW

Chair, MFA Design Criticism (D-Crit), School of Visual Arts, New York (Originally published in Eye *magazine, No. 80, Summer 2011)*

I've been writing about design since the winter of 1994. It was a piece about the mass-market graphic style of supermarket magazines like *Women's Own*, *Hello*, and *TV Times* in issue 15 of *Eye* that did it. It made me realize there was a publishing context for the kind of writing and the kind of subject matter that I was interested in.

I can picture the layout of the article, with its magenta titles on a brash red background and the covers of the featured magazines, all practically identical. Despite having moved continents since then, and offices several times, I know exactly where on my shelves to find that issue.

In 1994, I was a history of design student at the V&A Museum. Through studying history and connoisseurship I was beginning to realize I wanted to focus on the contemporary and the everyday. My research on the design of club and rave flyers was unusual in that context—willful even. At the V&A it was more common to write about 18th century chairs, gas lighting, or corsets. So the piece in Eye 15 by Keith Robertson, with its cool, non-judgmental analysis of supermarket tabloids, really struck a chord. When Robertson wrote that, "[mass-market graphic design's] conventions are instantly understood by its readers, yet like the black sheep of the typography family, it is a phenomenon that most design discussion ignores," he flagged a conundrum I still find compelling: the kind of design that is part of most people's lives is constitutionally incompatible with the design that designers and design writers talk about. Never mind a black sheep, mass-market design might as well be from another planet as far as most designers and design writers

are concerned. They raid it occasionally for ironic effect and comedic punch-line material, but don't give it serious consideration. And yet here was someone writing about "noisy," "aggressive," "value-for-money" graphics in the best-respected graphic design journal. Robertson's article set a challenge and showed a way forward for this fledgling design journalist.

Another essay which has become a touchstone for me and which was also written in 1994 is "Clip Art," by the author Nicholson Baker. Baker describes in intricate detail the design, production, evolution, marketing, use, and social implications of the ninety-nine-cent chrome-plated nail clipper. Baker's interest in the neglected aspects of life is well known and "Clip Art" was written as a riposte to a comment made by the author Stephen King, who had described one of Baker's books as "a meaningless little fingernail paring." Baker took King's slight as a challenge and, after his enthusiastic explication of the clippers, he went on to invoke a stream of literary references to fingernail parings, ranging from Norse myth to Joyce and Nabokov. For these writers, as for Baker, the humdrum objects, the overlooked fragments and marginalia of everyday life are more than background distraction; they are the very source and location of meaning. Investigating and analyzing the everyday is a line of cultural and critical enquiry that connects a lineage of writers who wish to resist their era's dominant and hegemonic mode of thought. For design critics, too, the choice of the everyday, the mass-produced, and the popular as subject matter is a way of reshaping the design canon and democratizing discussion about design.

Since then, design of the everyday has been further legitimized as subject matter both in publishing and in museums. MoMA's 2004 "Humble Masterpieces" show refocused attention toward the quiet brilliance of the Post-it note, paperclip, and Bic biro; the Walker Art Center's 2003 exhibition "Strangely Familiar: Design and Everyday Life" examined design's relationship to what Georges Perec has called "the banal, the obvious, the common, the ordinary, the infraordinary, the background noise, the habitual"; and club flyers are now a part of the V&A's collecting plan. My own interest in the material culture of the quotidian has continued unabated; I've written about the New York Greek Deli coffee cup, street stenciling, walk/don't walk sign interventions, Amazon product reviews, and the IKEA cafeteria.

You would have thought that blogs would have afforded regular and mass-market design more analysis and interpretation; that the cups, key rings, lotto cards, Hallmark cards, and Angry Birds Rios of our lives would have been contemplated and their implications discussed. And yet, all the blogs seem to do is to document and catalogue images of these things. Lists and collections, or what Rob Walker describes as "online projects devoted exclusively to lovely photographs of carefully arranged groups of objects," don't convey meaning, don't contribute to design discourse. What is still needed, I feel, and even more now in the wake of so many design magazine implosions, is well-written and well-edited feature articles that probe a subject and extract its significance, combined with tested techniques of art direction such as editorial pacing and multiple images, which allow a story to develop and intensify over several pages. News, reviews, profiles and captioned images have survived the migration to blogs and are flourishing; feature articles have been dispossessed, and I miss them.

%ₐ Alice Twemlow Talks about Covering Design Culture

What can we gain from looking at "mass-market"/ordinary design?

Bringing the entire critical tool set to bear on mass market or everyday design expands, enriches, and enlivens design discourse and benefits both people in the upper echelons of design commentary, like curators, academics, and editors, and people usually not particularly interested in design. Weekly entertainment magazines, mobile or social networking games like Angry Birds or Farmville, fast food packaging, or DMV license application forms are the kinds of design most people have contact with; providing them with the means for understanding them, talking about them usefully, and demanding better benefits everyone. By subjecting mass-market design to rigorous and scholarly interrogation and through the telling of compelling stories about it, you can also reach design's power brokers and help them have a better understanding of the scale and impact of contemporary social phenomena and design's role within them. This can help them make their own exhibitions, publications, and syllabi more relevant and likely to engage more people.

What are the advantages and drawbacks of writing about contemporary design culture?

It's important to write about contemporary design culture in order to separate what's harmful and wasteful from what's meaningful and valuable in real time so that your evaluation can actually have a chance of making a difference. Writing about contemporary design culture is liberating, because you can define the field on your own terms. There are no set canons, no established conventions; every aspect of contemporary design culture—from the material manifestations of Occupy Wall Street protests to graphic designers' current interest in performance as a strategy, and from an infectious trend such as "design thinking" to Snooki's style choices—is up for grabs as topics for inquiry. The challenge of working with this kind of material is, of course, that it doesn't sit still for analysis and evaluation; it is constantly changing, and as a critic you have to be able to make judgments in haste as well as knowing when exactly is the right moment to intervene and write something. As a critic you are a bit like a fly fisherman with a river of fish constantly flowing toward you. Which ones will you pick out to focus your attention on and when? Design history, on the other hand, gives you time.

for reflection, as well as neatly prescribed archives to work with and a body of literature dealing with your topic to consult. The other main advantage of design history to a writer is the fact that your subjects can't talk back or be offended by your critique. Writing about contemporary design culture often means having to go head to head with individuals who you consider to be implicated in harmful or inane design activity; that's tough for everyone involved, but absolutely necessary for the evolution of a robust and publicly useful design-critical literature.

Who do you write for, when writing design criticism?

I love this question because it's one I'm obsessed with. I think writers often have the sensation of writing into a vacuum and not knowing if their words have hit home in any meaningful way. I'm a Ph.D. candidate at the RCA and my research examines the dynamics of design criticism in the United Kingdom and the United States since the 1950s, focusing on design criticism's relationship to its publics, which include designers, manufacturers, consumers, and policy makers. Throughout my project I am interested in the impact of, or response to, design criticism—how its provocations are met, received, and acted upon by their audiences in a kind of critical circuitry. So I'm looking at letters in magazines and newspapers, comments on blogs, customer responses to Amazon product reviews, visitor comments at exhibitions, and audience feedback at conferences which, in the case of the 1970 Aspen Design Conference, took the form of student protests which forced a change of direction in the following conferences.

What do you say to your students?

With my students at D-Crit I'm constantly posing them with the challenge of how to engage the broadest possible audience in the deepest implications of design. We spend a good deal of time becoming proficient in different media—different carriers of criticism such as radio, documentary, exhibitions, and even animation, book clubs, or boat tours, and exploring how they might help us engage our audiences. I'm currently excited by the potential of the VH1 Pop Up Video format for design criticism.

And who are you writing for?

In abstract terms, I am writing for a rather eclectic dinner party of readers—I can almost see them awkwardly gathered around a table together—which includes the designer Michael Bierut, whose Geiger counter for nonsense is so finely tuned; Reyner Banham, the late design critic and historian who is my hero in terms of writing, subject matter, and approach; author and sometime design critic Nicholson Baker; my Mum, who needs to be able to summarize the gist of the piece to her friends in the village; the cab driver I spent last night's trip home trying to convince what was so important about design; my Ph.D. supervisors David Crowley and Jeremy Aynsley; as well as the protagonists in the story, be they the designers, manufacturers, or other decision makers involved in the project under discussion. No wonder I never feel satisfied with my writing!

In more specific terms, with each commission I'll try to picture a typical member of its likely readership—a general interest piece in *New York* magazine demands a perky, authoritative tone designed to catch the attention of a reader who is standing up on a subway train while texting and checking out the guy who just stepped into her carriage, and has only a passing interest in design. A piece in an academic journal should be written to last—with attitude, but not in a style so pronounced that it doesn't bear rereading—for a young curator who can actually put my research to some good use.

Where can we find good writing on popular design?

Historically, the founding father of this type of writing is Reyner Banham, who redefined the scope of design criticism in the 1960s by treating artifacts of everyday experience such as crisp packets, surfboards, ice cream trucks, and sheriff's badges with the same seriousness as canonized design. He wrote columns in general interest magazines such as *New Society* and *New Statesman* in the late 1950s and 1960s, and made his subject matter so accessible and his critical process so visible that he empowered the casual observer to comment on their own designed environment. Today, you can find good writing about popular design amongst Amazon product reviews, as I have discussed in a piece published on *Design Observer*, but in general you really have to search for it in novels, in the pages of The *New Yorker* or The *London Review of Books*, or in online columns of *The Atlantic Cities*.

What skills should one actively cultivate for good design writing?

Most of the qualities I value in good design writing are the same as those necessary for good writing about anything: humor; a good sense of rhythm and pacing; a playful relationship to language; engaging narrative with a killer first paragraph; a clear sense of the writer's stance and perspective; excellent reporting which highlights all kinds of details only accessible through face-to-face interviewing over time; the canny knack for identifying a good story and the social adroitness to get access to its main players; deep historical knowledge both in terms of the subject matter, but also in terms of other pieces written about this subject; and razor-sharp analytical skills.

The writer who specializes in design also needs to have some other qualities, and these include the ability to see, to really see, design, and unpack the layers of its production and intentionality for the benefit of the reader. I would argue that all of these skills can be acquired, provided the student is prepared to embark on a lifelong project of learning and relearning. The one aspect of design writing I really struggle with, in terms of how it might be cultivated—is taste. An unfashionable subject, of course, and one that you might think is at odds with my deep interest in the everyday, and yet I believe it underpins good writing about design just as an unplaceable spice—an ineffable flavor—makes a good dish sublime. How to discriminate between what is good and bad aesthetically can be developed through practice, I suppose, but learned taste does not have the same dimensionality or plausibility as its near relative, which is taste that is innate, felt, lived, and inescapable.

3 BUSINESS

Business writing comes in many forms (no pun intended): very officious, somewhat officious, less officious, and all the nuances in between. Many handbooks and guides have been published on the craft of writing acceptable business communications. I prefer *The Graphic Design Business Book* by Tad Crawford because it situates business text in the context of practice. But virtually any book or website that summarizes how to communicate with clients, prospective clients, and the public will do just as nicely. The key to this genre of writing is balance.

The "voice," which I've touted as essential to good writing, is not to be overdone in business writing. Still, some of the other tenets are. Know who you are writing for (whether you're writing a letter, proposal, report, etc.). Maintain a tone that does not drown the reader with jargon or presuppose the reader's ignorance. Intelligence, brevity, even a modicum of wit is essential for good business communications. With that as a guideline,

common sense should prevail. This is a case where the facts and "nothing but the facts" is a pretty good mantra.

The following essay by the design writing eminence, Ralph Caplan, about ordinary language and writing skill, can be applied throughout this book. But as a primer for writing about the design business, it is inspired. Read and learn.

CASE STUDY:

ORN'RY USAGE

RALPH CAPLAN

Ralph Caplan is the author of By Design *and* Cracking the Whip.
(Originally published April 6, 2011 on AIGA Journal, *www.aiga.org/ornry-usage/)*

Everyone who cares about language has a list of personal offenses. Among mine are *irregardless* for *regardless*, *lay* for *lie*, *like* for *as*, *criteria* for *criterion*, *less* for *fewer*, plus words or phrases that are superfluous because we already have adequate ways of saying the same thing.

Expertness, for example, was always a perfectly good expression. *Expertise* adds nothing more but a suffix with pretentious roots. *At this point in time* is no improvement on *now*, but sounds more precise and scholarly; perhaps it originally entered the language as a way of distinguishing time from space.

Between you and I makes me cringe, suspecting that the speaker learned (or thought she learned) from a grade school English teacher that *I* is right and *me* wrong, and has ever since felt secure only by avoiding *me* whenever possible.

Rules are not really made to be broken; however, they are designed to be breakable. Many of us have our favorite violations. Steve Heller, the dean of design writers, refuses to stop using *irregardless*, even though he knows there is no such word, "because I like the irrrrrr sound." As for me, I happily give poetry a pass. One of my favorite hymns is the so-called "white spiritual" "I Wonder as I Wander," with lyrics that ask plaintively:

Why did the Lord Jesus come down for to die
For poor orn'ry sinners like you and like I?

That doesn't make me cringe, but it would if corrected. The solecism, forced by rhyme, is beautiful there. Allegiance to grammar would ruin it. So I have to remind myself not only that rules can be broken, but that language, being alive, changes. But while we know that language changes, we don't always know when it's happening. An exception—a change occurring before our very ears—is the tendency to use a singular verb in a contraction, even when the noun is plural.

"There's three preferred typefaces." That's not a genuine quote, because I don't know that anyone has said it. But if someone had, it wouldn't have bothered us much. On the other hand, people have said: "There's three reporters on every story"; "There's a great many things for Obama to consider"; "There's several problems with nuclear energy"; "There's two bills on the table"; "There's a few ways of looking at this"; "There's too many things going on right now."

That doesn't trouble us either, and I guarantee you'll hear the locution today if you listen to the radio, watch TV, attend a meeting, or talk to a neighbor. The speakers you will hear it from are not illiterate. They would never say, "There is too many things going on." But verbs in those ungrammatical examples are all contractions, making the breach of grammar acceptable. Why? Maybe because, when speaking, it is easy to forget how a sentence began. I think it more likely, though, that it represents the present tendency to relax formal standards in language, whether written or spoken.

Should any of this concern designers? At first it may not seem so. But, after all, graphic designers devised standards manuals to keep corporations from violating the structure created for them. Long before that, usage manuals for writers were created for somewhat comparable reasons. Because language changes, the manuals do too, becoming updated almost as soon as they are printed, raising the question of why they should be printed at all. (They may not be for much longer.)

The best-known and most popular contemporary usage manual is *The Elements of Style*, E. B. White's revision of the textbook written by his college English professor William Strunk. The book's popularity stems from White's highly reasoned updating and his loving description of encounters with the book and author. I love reading it, and when asked by students to recommend a manual, I encourage them to buy Strunk and White's book in the 2007 edition enhanced by Maira Kalman's splendid, wayward art, because it is a book they will love and should own. But I suggest that they use whatever manual is used by the school they attend or the company they work for, which is likely to be either the manual of the University of Chicago or The *New York Times*, and to turn to the Internet for anything more recent.

In a talk to SVA students recently, Michael Bierut pointed out that design has moved from an exclusive concern with the appearance of type on a page, to participation in content. Certainly the design community is richly loaded with designers whose writing matches the standard of their graphics—Bierut himself, Milton Glaser, Bill Drenttel, Paula Scher, Maira Kalman, Ellen Lupton, Abbott Miller, Lorraine Wild, Brad Holland, and many others.

While standards are less rigid than they once were, even in an age of texting and tweeting they are still essential to designers of communication. Because words express content, certain principles of construction are necessary to frame their delivery. At the very least we need an armature to support ideas until they are stable enough to make sense on their own. Even if it must in the end be discarded. Like the goldsmith's wax, rules may not just be broken, but lost.

Otherwise we're condemned to a world of poor orn'ry sinners like you and like me.

Ⓠ/Ⓐ Ralph Caplan Talks about Writing Skill

Why do you feel it behooves a designer to develop good writing skills?

For the same reason it behooves anyone else to develop them: Life goes better for those who can communicate clearly. But designers in particular need such skills because so much of design is itself a form of communication. Also, design today invariably involves collaboration. That means participation in meetings, an activity in which persuasive clarity is almost as useful as obfuscation.

Who exemplifies this and why?

As my "Orn'ry Usage" piece points out, many graphic designers do. Two I didn't mention are Jessica Helfand and Deborah Sussman. Many product designers do as well—Gianfranco Zaccai, and the late Bill Stumpf, for example—and architects, partly because they are more likely to have been educated traditionally. This is especially important because the design process, for reasons I deplore, requires continual explanation.

Do you generally write for the ear or the eye?

Both. Most readers are equipped with both, and assimilate information through whatever organs are available for the task. In his commencement address at Stanford, Steve Jobs attributed much of his personal style to the calligraphy and fonts he encountered in the only formal class he took at Reed College. So he knew the importance of a sensitive eye. Poets like Dylan Thomas and Theodore Roethke acknowledged the role of sound in their writing. So they were aware of how much comes in by ear.

How useful is humor as a writing tool?

As a rule, if it is seen as a tool, humor is more dangerous than useful. The weakest speakers are those who think a joke is always helpful as an instrument for winning over an audience. Humor is generally effective when used by writers who are genuinely funny. Everyone who has successfully written humorously, from Mark Twain to Nora Ephron, has been able to do so because humor is intrinsic to their personalities and their work. Designers like Milton Glaser, Paula Scher, and Maira Kalman are able to incorporate humor into what they write and say because they don't have to; it is naturally part of their content. Tools are devices used for particular jobs. Humor is, or isn't, part of who we are.

What traits should a design writer have that may be unique to the genre of design writing?

I don't think any are unique to design writing, but some are more important in that field than in others. All writers should strive, as Henry James urged, to "try to be one of those on whom nothing is lost," but the admonition is especially pertinent to writing about design. Noticing details is crucial. Design writers need to be especially sensitive to how things are made and to how they look, and to the relationship between the two.

④ ACADEMIC

Scholarly writing has gotten something of a bum rap, particularly as it applies to design writing. For decades, architecture monographs were written more as brain drains than as prose poems—they tend to be streams of historical, critical, and anecdotal consciousness. When designers began to write in a scholarly and critical manner, this model was often followed. The discipline has improved greatly since the early days when design writing was either overly "trade" or oppressively "academic" (think jargon, footnotes, and lots of substantiating quotations).

When I started writing in the late seventies, I adopted a seriously serious tone influenced by the anthropology papers my then-wife wrote when she was a doctoral candidate. She would edit my texts and insert words that were not mine (like mode and paradigm) but sounded viable—and intelligent—so I retained them. In fact, I would insert them when I wanted to make some design trope or mannerism appear a significant "mode" of expression. I will admit it gave me a certain level of credibility, although people who read my work often said, "We expected you were much, much older." The caricaturist, Ed Sorel, himself an entertaining and fluid author, chided me for "writing like Charles Dickens." In other words, I found it difficult to be loose. And that is because I enjoyed reading back my texts and thinking "this guy is so smart." This fallacy ended when my wife and I divorced—I got the apartment and the car; she took the cat and the scholarly words and phrases.

Still, academic writing demands certain rigors that are not routine in more journalistic prose. Presumably, an academic work is a more thorough report, analysis, and telling of the subject. Footnotes or internal reference notes are compulsory to not only show where the scholar's ideas derived, but also guide readers to additional information or even contradictory positions. But even more than footnotes, scholarship demands that every stone is unturned to become expert in your field, and that must be apparent through how the text is structured to answer even the unasked questions.

In the following case study, by Kerry William Purcell, the author of professional biographical monographs on the art director Alexey Brodovitch and Swiss design pioneer Josef Müller-Brockmann, very important and all-but-forgotten English design magazines are historically recalled. Although Purcell does not use footnotes, the authority of his voice is bolstered by relevant dates and outside quotations. His decided mastery of historical fact contributes to the credibility. This essay, which has been excerpted, serves as a resource for others interested in this specific subject, or like me, in the overall history of design magazines.

CASE STUDY:

EXCERPTS FROM *ALPHABET AND IMAGE*

KERRY WILLIAM PURCELL

Kerry William Purcell is a lecturer in design history at The University of Hertfordshire. Originally published in Baseline #50, 2006

British graphic design was a profession in search of an identity in 1945. As with most occupations, war had marked an unyielding pause in the workaday routines of the industry.

During this period the obligations and urgency of conflict had called for the production of posters, pamphlets and publications that, by necessity, demanded a simple graphic immediacy. Whether through the use of typography in mass propaganda, or photography in the Royal Society for the Prevention of Accident (RoSPA) posters, a softened modernism had proved its worth for a newly emerging group of young designers. It would be a mistake, however, to imply that the design landscape ensuing from this period was changed radically after 1945. On returning to their duties, many printers and designers were quick to realise that while many other industries had exploited the new practices and technologies brought about by wartime innovation, the post-war design world was still dominated by an earlier generation of conservative typographers and craftsmen. Changing from military attire to civilian suit, the young typographer or designer was also required to don a willful ignorance toward the extensive possibilities peacetime afforded.

One figure who attempted to bridge the gap between the earlier artist-craftsman of the twenties and thirties and the new post-war graphic designer was Robert Harling. Born in 1910 in Highbury, London, Harling was educated in Brighton and London, before attending the Central School of Arts and Crafts. Soon after completion of his studies he quickly established himself as a significant figure in the British design scene. Alongside design work at the *Daily Mail*, he occupied

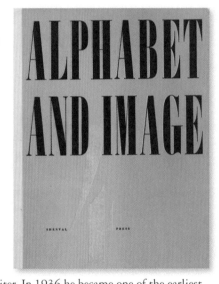

key advisory roles at London Transport and the celebrated Sheffield-based foundry Stephenson Blake & Co., where he also supplied the new typefaces Playbill (1938), Chisell (1939) and Tea Chest (1939).

Harling's abilities as a designer were more than equaled by his talents as a writer. In 1936 he became one of the earliest critics to familiarize the English design world with the work of Jan Tschichold in his essay 'What is this "Functional" typography? The work of Jan Tschichold in Printing' (even if he did later charge Tschichold's early work as 'really too refrigerated and mathematical to be true'). It was in this same year that Harling brought his combined experience of designer-writer to bear on the founding of *Typography*. The origins of this influential quarterly magazine (originally published in an edition of 1,200) came through Harling's association with the printer James Shand (and to a lesser degree, Eric Howe). Together with Shand, Harling set out to create a publication that encompassed a mixture of historical features on rarely examined areas of graphic art, alongside articles that assessed more recent typographical developments. By focusing concurrently on popular design ephemera and groundbreaking new works, both editor and publisher were ahead of their time in forgoing any distinction between the products of high and low culture. 'The sponsors of *Typography* believe that fine book production is not the only means of typographical expression or excitement', they assured the reader. 'We believe, in fact that a bill-head can be as aesthetically pleasing as a Bible, that a newspaper can be as typographically arresting as a Nonesuch.' Thus, alongside features showcasing the designs of E. McKnight Kauffer, Herbert Bayer, Eric Gill, and Jan Tschichold, we also find examples of tea label and tram ticket designs. It was a mixture of the traditional and modern that was echoed in Harling's covers for the magazine, which frequently utilised a variety of geometrical elements combined with an eclectic mix of distinguished typefaces. The publication was also bound in a radical plastoic spiral. The decision to use this relatively unconventional bind was that it allowed the editors to include essays and reproductions printed via contrasting processes and on differing papers. Another benefit was that the spiral bind

↑ Cover of *Alphabet and Image* #5.

ℚ/ⓐ Kerry William Purcell Talks about Writing History

Lecturer in design history, the University of Hertfordshire

How much critical or interpretive leeway do you allow when writing history?

Beyond the key dates and individuals involved, it's all critical and interpretive leeway! As I've discovered with most of my writing, I simply follow the inclinations and associations specific material objects may set off in my mind. Of course, there needs to be a bedrock of historical understanding, but let's not kid ourselves, we are drawn to subjects, and we make the connections we think are important. We can offer an argument for the points we make and try to convince others (I'm certainly not a relativist!), but we should not hide behind some supposedly objective façade.

Where and how do you do your research?

My research is conducted in such places as the National Art Library (at the Victoria and Albert Museum) and online. But most of the links and connecting threads that enable me to develop an essay come when I'm swimming, just drifting off to sleep, or driving back and forth to my university.

How much of your research is primary (i.e., records from A + I) or secondary (previously recorded history or commentary)?

It's a mix of both. I wished I could have spoken to Robert Harling (he died two years after this article was published), but the occasion did not present itself.

How would you, if at all, revise this essay, and why?

No, I am quite happy with it as it is. I very rarely read through an old essay. Maybe my approach is equivalent to the way many designers are with projects, in that once I have finished it, I just move on to the next thing. Even when I get the published version, I won't reread it. Actually, I have numerous packages containing copies of magazines that have articles by me in them, which I have not even opened. I'm not sure why this is, but I just think that I've spent enough time on it and I don't really have the desire to see it again.

↑ Spread from *Alphabet and Image* on the mastheads of 18th-century newspapers.

allowed the magazine to be laid flat when being read. Altogether, this synthesis of form and content made *Typography* into one of the most significant and sought after English design publications of the 1930s.

Typography ran for only eight issues. As events in Europe began to impinge upon the daily routines of the nation, Harling and Shand's publication schedule began to falter and issue number seven was delayed. Eventually published in the winter of 1938, an apology for this delay was expressed in issue number eight. However, rather optimistically, the editors noted in the summer 1939 edition that the magazine would continue to be published on a quarterly basis. Any realisation of this timetable was quashed when on 3 September 1939 Britain and France declared war on Nazi Germany.

Harling played his role in the conflict and enlarged upon his wartime experiences in two highly praised books. As the late

Ruari McLean noted, 'among other things, [Harling] was also a weekend sailor, and took part in the Dunkirk operation, which he described in *Amateur Sailor*, [which] appeared in 1944 [published by Constable] under the pen-name Nicholas Drew, a book which John Masefield said was the best eye witness account of it ever written.' Following this he 'joined the Navy, served in the corvettes, and described that in [the book] *Steep Atlantick Stream*,' published by Chatto & Windus in 1946. 'He was then called into naval intelligence, under Admiral Godfrey, and worked with Ian Fleming, who became his close friend.'

Upon resumption of his civilian duties, Harling continued to combine the careers of writer and designer. His articles appeared in both trade publications and newspapers, while his design commissions included work for *Time & Tide*, *Art & Industry* and *The Sunday Times*. It was in the spring of

1946 that he decided to resume publication of *Typography*. However, both Harling and Shand considered the original title too limiting for the diverse range of visual material they had regularly featured in this quarterly. The new title of *Alphabet and Image* was deemed more fitting of a publication that would often include between the same covers an essay on the work of a celebrated illustrator, an article on fat typefaces, and analysis of the newspaper printing industry. As both editor and publisher remarked in the first issue:

'We sometimes thought *Typography* a limiting title, and, almost in defianceof that label, published several contributions not strictly typographical...

Alphabet and Image will, from its earliest days avoid any hint of such limitation. Under its simple but flexible title it is hoped that an appraisal of an eighteenth-century draughtsman or a contemporary photographer may be included as naturally and logically as a review of a recent typeface or reproductions of antique penmanship.'

With this broadening of its editorial focus, Harling and Shand wished to make it clear that *Alphabet and Image* (*A & I*) would not relinquish its aim of covering all that was best in typography and the graphic arts. 'Every endeavour', they continued, 'will be made to keep their magazine from slipping into one of the two fates which seem inevitably to await almost every current English magazine: (a) trying to be the English *Fortune*; (b) becoming a literary publication.' Both editors concluded their opening introduction recounting that 'many in this country and abroad, particularly the United States, were kind in comment concerning their earlier venture. Others were critical. It is thought that the characteristics which provoked these comments are likely to be found in a more emphatic degree in *Alphabet and Image*. Brickbats and bouquets are solicited.'

Published by Shand's Shenval Press, *A & I* measured 19.5 cm x 24.5 cm and continued to use the distinctive plasticol binding employed in *Typography*. The first issue has a cover design by Harling that employs a two-colour letterpress. The 'T' of *Alphabet* creatively bisects the 'A' of *And*, with the issue number '1' overlapping the 'E' of *Image*. As with *Typography*, the striking cover designs of *A & I* encapsulated the diversity

of influences sought by Harling. Throughout all his designs, a mixture of the ornate and modern in both type and number were playfully married with an imaginative use of colour. This contrast set the tone for the content, which opened with an analysis upon the numbering of newspapers by Stanley Morison and a feature on the illustrations of Mervyn Peake. We then have an early article by Ruari McLean on Egyptian typefaces, which is accompanied by an essay on the type designer Edward Johnston and notes on a centenary event for the children's book illustrator Kate Greenaway. The 'Notes' section towards the rear kept the reader up-to-date with events, publications and latest news from the graphic arts world. This format of five to seven articles, with an addendum, remained the same throughout all issues of *A & I*.

Harling's decision to re-launch *Typography* as *A & I* in 1946 was, as we have seen, partially determined by the need to address the lack of communication across the printing and design professions. The absence of consultation and a shared knowledge base was frustrating the development of an industry at a time of expansion. By situating articles on illustrators alongside those examining print history and type design, Harling clearly perceived *A & I* as having an important pedagogic role to play in enabling a culture of debate and cross fertilisation. Unfortunately, by 1948 this experiment had seemingly failed. The printing industry appeared unwilling to enter into any discussion regarding the creative possibilities of working closely with designers and illustrators. The eighth issue of *A & I* was the last (all eight issues of the quarterly were lately anthologised and re-published by Harling in 1975). In Harling's final editorial he noted that 'with this issue. . . this magazine ends its days. *Alphabet* will live again, subtitled *An Annual of Typography*, and the first volume will be published in autumn 1949. The first number of *Image*, subtitled *A Quarterly of the Arts*, will be published in spring 1949....' Harling continues:

'The study of typography is an increasingly popular subject, but it remains a specialized division of design and the number of potential readers of a publication concerned with the subject is limited. We are persuaded, therefore, that we can employ ourselves more usefully by dealing in a more specialized manner with the typographical subjects and by dealing with the arts which have become more popular in recent years on a much broader basis than we have in *Alphabet and Image.*

In its exceptional range and quality of work, *A & I* embodied Harling's belief 'that the chief value of anything designed was the pleasure it gave to the designer.' The publication also existed as an example of his claim that good writing, whether commercial copy or historical analysis, was an essential component of the design process. Through this mixture of skillful design and intelligent writing, Harling attempted to meet the needs of a new reader: the graphic designer. In its anticipation of this new role *A & I* was ahead of its time. Yet, this was also to be the source of its demise. At the beginning of this new era, the graphic designer remained a rare commodity, one unable to offer a sizable enough audience to sustain this important quarterly magazine. Even so, in both text and image, Harling's experiment endures as a formative work in the development of post-war English design.

Q/A Linda King Talks about Scholarly Writing

Linda King is a lecturer in design history, theory, and visual communication at the Institute of Art, Design and Technology in Dublin, Ireland.

You have written for a scholarly and academic audience. What are the characteristics that separate academic from mainstream writing about design?

That's a really interesting question. I suppose the main difference with writing for an academic audience is that you assume your audience will have some prior knowledge of your themes or frames of reference. This allows you to deepen the arguments more quickly and to expand on why something has happened in a particular way, at a particular time, and what can be learned from that experience. You are, in effect, writing for an audience, which have done a little more "homework" than most other people.

Do you believe that academic or historical writing about design must be filled with jargon?

The challenge, as I see it, is more about the appropriate use of language and clarity of expression. There are certain words or phrases that are typical of academic writing which may not have common currency, but which are useful in nuancing and clarifying certain arguments. I think you can use less well-known terminology, if it's appropriate to making your point, without losing your audience. One of the most wonderful qualities of the English language is that there are so many words that are slight variations on each other in terms of meaning; this allows authors to be very exact in what they want to say. Coincidently, I'm currently rereading *A Clockwork Orange* after first having read it thirty years ago. Part of the joy of reading this book is trying to decipher the language Anthony Burgess invented—Nadsat—without having to resort to a glossary for explanation. I know this is an extreme example of how language is manipulated, but the use of this subcultural language is totally appropriate in the context of the book and enhances the narrative even if you don't understand every word. That said, I do get irritated when writers consciously overcomplicate their writing for the sake of appearing more scholarly, particularly when the idea is very simple to begin with!

As a scholar do you tend to write for other scholars?

When I'm researching and writing I assume that the main audiences for my work are students, scholars, and designers interested in where design and cultural history intersect. My primary motivation is as a teacher, and so I'm constantly trying to provide "useful" sources for students in thinking about designed objects and visual culture. However, I'm always conscious, and constantly reminded, that my primary area of research—the design strategies of Aer Lingus, the former Irish national airline—is of interest to a much broader audience. The story of Aer Lingus is so integral to Irish history and cultural identity that my work is often discovered by people outside of the worlds of design and academia, and I find that very rewarding. Aer Lingus has a Forest Gump-like quality in that its planes and staff are visibly present in the photographs and film footage of many key historical moments in Irish history, including the visits of JFK in 1963, Che Guevara in 1964, Muhammad Ali in 1972, and Pope John Paul II in 1979. The patronage of Aer Lingus was also key in promoting many areas of Irish design, including graphic, industrial, fashion, and textile design. I really enjoy researching a subject that many people can relate to on a variety of different levels.

What is your favorite sentence?

Hand on heart I am never happy with anything I write. When I was working as a graphic designer I was never happy with anything I designed either! But the [endeavor] for perfection—which of course is unobtainable—makes you try harder each time.

⑤ CRITICISM

A serious design criticism and history discipline was born in 1983 at the first R.I.T. Design History Symposium. Over the past decades, various symposia, numerous books, and diverse articles, papers, and courses of study have emerged. The scholarship has matured far beyond the early slide shows of classic works by patriarchal pioneers into a broad and rich collection of genres, forms, and individuals who directly and indirectly contribute to the popular culture.

Criticism expands knowledge by revealing otherwise hidden meanings. The so-called "positive" method examines a maker's intent and rationale; a work's structure is scrutinized and the factors that inform it are contextualized, providing the basis for balanced analysis and historical categorization. Conversely, the so-called "negative" method is a kind of fault-finding exposé of flaws in a process or result. The purpose is ostensibly to reinforce a set of standards used to judge success or failure. Both methods are useful in addressing the form and function of design.

Until recently graphic design, whether a total identity system or an individual poster, has been immune from the kind of public scrutiny given books, films, plays, painting, and sculpture, even advertising. Graphic design has been seen but not heard about. Only those media that are directly marketed to the public and play a more integral cultural role are given a spot in the critical limelight. In the past, graphic design was not criticizable because authorship was comparatively invisible and, moreover, design routinely served a supporting role. There was also a gentleman's agreement within the graphic design community that a demonstrative critical voice was simply unnecessary.

Distinctions within the field between good and bad design were pronounced through the results of art directors' competitions where the reasons for inclusion or exclusion were rarely articulated. Other than the positive reinforcement of winning a medal, designers were not held individually accountable. Seldom, therefore, was an individual graphic designer's body of work critical grist. Along the way a critical language has developed to help put these phenomena in context, suggest values and standards, and question assumptions. Criticism is a very positive means of illuminating—the warts and all—a design work, genre, or phenomenon.

Rick Poynor, founding editor of *Eye* magazine, and one of the pioneer graphic design critics, has long written on the role of the critic and the impact of criticism. Here he delves into a theme that has underscored his work of more than two decades. Read it closely to see how he develops his argument and attempts to convince his readers.

CASE STUDY:

THE DEATH OF THE CRITIC

RICK POYNOR

Rick Poynor is the founding editor of Eye *magazine. (Originally published in* Icon, *March 2006)*

Does design criticism matter anymore? It's certainly not a term you hear bandied about by designers. Busy professionals have clients to meet, projects to plan, studios to run. If designers were to think about design criticism at all, they {would} probably imagine that it is still going on somewhere—and good luck to it.

But if we aren't actively looking for design criticism, how do we know whether it's flourishing or not? There is plenty of design journalism, but criticism and journalism are different activities. While it's certainly possible for journalism to have a critical intention, most design journalism simply reports on the latest news. There is nothing wrong with that, but it isn't criticism and it tells us nothing about criticism's state of health.

We will call design criticism in for a fitness check and take its pulse in due course, but first it might be useful to look at what criticism is for. These tasks aren't specific to design criticism. They also apply, in differing degrees, to the criticism of cultural activities such as art, architecture, literature and film.

Perhaps the most basic service provided by criticism has been to champion the new. The idea here is that without the intervention of the critic, the public would fail to understand or appreciate artistic innovations. People might ignore or even attack them. The critic is presumed to have special insight into the motivations and meaning of the work that comes from a deep personal engagement. It may be necessary to challenge earlier ways of thinking to explain why these creations are timely and significant. The critic may become strongly identified with particular individuals, movements or causes, a fellow traveller with the innovators he champions,

influencing their artistic development and ideas.

If we consider this model in terms of contemporary design, some problems emerge. Most obviously, there is no public resistance to design today and there is no provocative design avant-garde requiring the critic to step in as intermediary and advocate. Twenty-five years ago, Memphis might have needed this kind of critical support. The movement was controversial with modernist designers, and writers trotted out various theories to explain it. Where are the contemporary equivalents? Postmodern design caused a ruckus for a while, but this passed and nothing as turbulent has occurred since then. Meanwhile, adventurous design has become something that any modern consumer appreciates. People need updates about the latest sofas, mobile phones, bars, restaurants and hip hotels, but they don't need anyone to argue the case for these things or to explain their relevance. Journalism handles the publicity— from the glossy interior mags to reports in the daily press.

The same reservation applies to criticism's more general function of promoting a discipline's cause. Fifty years ago, design needed all the support it could get. "The role of the serious critic is that of an educator," wrote advertising designer Ashley Havinden in 1952. "By searching out the many examples of good design and appraising them constructively, he may convince the manufacturer or the printer of the merits of good design associated with his product....Such constructive criticism in the press would teach the public, not only to appreciate, but to demand good design in the products they buy." Today, we have plenty of organisations and initiatives to beat the drum for design: the Design Council, the British Council, D&AD, the London Design Festival. It's debatable whether writing produced for this well-worn purpose can be regarded as criticism.

The third possible function of criticism goes considerably further than mere promotion. This kind of writing takes design's presence for granted as something that no longer needs to be argued for, and it arises from a commitment to design's cultural possibilities. The emphasis here falls on the depth, subtlety, sophistication and complexity of the critic's response. The writing is more discursive and playful; it weaves around its subject; it offers pleasures of its own. Making assessments of quality might once have been a key task for this type of criticism, but this has become unfashionable in other art forms, particularly in visual art, and today it is less likely to be attempted in design writing, where there is an inherent tension between subjective aesthetic reactions and more objective assessments of whether or not a design fulfils its functional purpose. The problem with the more rarefied forms of criticism is that they can too easily seem to be arcane and elitist and, in the age of public access, this is unacceptable to many. Even art people seem to find much of what is written about art unreadable.

The final category of criticism takes a more questioning and sometimes even hostile view of the subject. This is the cultural studies approach. It treats cultural production as a form of evidence, taking these phenomena apart to discover what they reveal about society, and viewing the subject matter through particular lenses: feminism, racism, consumerism, sustainability. Design, as a primarily commercial endeavour, makes a particularly good subject for this type of analysis and unmasking. The problem, from a designer's point of view, is that this form of design commentary can be deeply sceptical about many things that a working professional takes for granted. Designers who read it are often confronted with two bald alternatives: feel bad about what you are doing or change your ways. Combative, campaigning criticism—Naomi Klein's *No Logo* is the best known recent example—is more likely to come from outside the design world.

This summary suggests some of the difficulties facing design criticism today. There are other factors that need to be taken into account. It has been publishing wisdom for years that readers' appetite to plough through long articles has dwindled. We are busier than ever, the thinking runs, and other forms of media compete for the browser's attention. Magazines respond with an easy to swallow diet of captions, sidebars and pictures. If criticism needs space to flex its muscles, then today's design magazines are not always eager to supply it. You can see this at work in the industry bible *Design Week*, never the most critical of organs. Since the magazine's redesign, which increased the page size, articles appear to be shorter, with smaller type that only adds to the feeling that the words take up space that might be better allotted to more colour pictures. The "Private View" opinion column was hardly an unduly taxing read at 800 words; it has been slashed to just 500.

The notion of criticism has been undermined in other ways. The critic, as traditionally understood, was a person of superior knowledge and insight. Critics presumed to know best about their areas of expertise. They made judgements on behalf of other people and their authoritative pronouncements about books, films or art used to count for something. New York theatre critics could famously close plays with a damning review. People are much less prepared now to regard critics as sources of authoritative opinion. A consumer guide with handy star ratings may be all you need to decide which CD to buy this week or which movie to see.

It's often said that everyone is a critic today and the Internet, with its challenge to all forms of printed authority, has taken this democracy of opinion to a new level. A growing army of bloggers offers commentary that editors would never dream of publishing in print on every aspect of cultural life. When everyone can broadcast their views so easily, the position of the critic looks much less distinctive and necessary. Still, the torrent of words unleashed by blogging and the popularity of some sites seem to contradict the idea that people are less prepared to read than they were.

Whether design criticism has a future or not, we should at least be clear about what it can do.

When it comes to design, it's sometimes suggested that blogs might offer a new forum for design criticism and, as a design writer, this certainly attracted me. In 2003, I co-founded a site called *Design Observer* with three American designers and for a couple of years I wrote short essays for it as often as I could. What I soon realised was that as a medium for writing (as opposed to more diary-like uses) blogging software is a kind of Trojan horse. The open-to-all-comers comment box at the end of each entry can generate a vast trail of digression that overpowers the original article, no matter how carefully it is written. One 1,000-word *Design Observer* essay by a colleague produced more than 60,000 words of comment—the size of a book—much of it utterly pointless. Internet publishing might, in time, provide a way forward for criticism, but I am not convinced that blogs will. Attempts to define a distinctive position disappear beneath the hubbub.

Whether design criticism has a future or not, we should at least be clear about what it can do. Here, I want to turn to an example that shows what critical thinking used to mean in the design field, and that suggests why we still need it today.

In June 1955, the *Architectural Review* published a special issue, written by the brilliant architecture critic Ian Nairn, then just 25, which it titled *Outrage*. The issue documents the spread of what the *AR* calls Subtopia—a compound of suburb and utopia—across Britain. "Subtopia," Nairn writes, "is the annihilation of the difference by attempting to make one type of scenery standard for town, suburb, countryside and wild." The *AR* documents this with great thoroughness. Everything about the issue—the use of drawings and different coloured papers, the typography—glows with visual intelligence. Nairn shows scores of photographs of street lamps, arterial roads, overhead wires, street advertising and bungled attempts at "municipal rustic". He undertakes a 400-mile car journey from Southampton to Carlisle, producing a written commentary

supported by pictures of everything he sees, then switches his attention to the Scottish Highlands, where he looks at housing, roads, tourism, hydro-electricity. The issue ends with a manifesto about what needs to be done aimed at the man in the street, which sets out some precepts ("The site's the thing, not a set of rules, and your eye's the thing, not the textbook") and offers a comprehensive list of malpractices to watch out for ("has the town lost its centre to the car park? or the open square to a wired-in public garden?").

What is remarkable about *Outrage* is its controlled anger and passion. The purpose of criticism here is to force open people's eyes, to change opinion and make a difference. The writer has a view of Subtopia grounded in a philosophical awareness of what it signifies for the person who lives inside it: "Insensible to the meaning of civilization on the one side and, on the other, ignorant of the well-spring of his own being, he is removing the sharp edge from his own life, exchanging individual feeling for mass experience in a voluntary enslavement far more restrictive and permanent than the feudal system." The issue became a book and it's clear from the many reviews quoted on the cover that it received a level of attention in the papers that a design magazine initiative would never be granted today. "Sameness can become a most virulent form of ugliness," writes *The Observer*. "If we are not shocked into recognising it in time, we shall ourselves become subtopians, sub-humans, no longer individuals but forever members of a herd."

To produce a scorching critique like this you need profound idealism and a shared sense of what matters and we have lost this now. Much of what Nairn and the *AR* feared came to pass in spite of their protests. In their terms, the visual environment of Britain was carelessly ruined. Subtopia—sprawl, if you prefer—continues to throw a dull blanket of sameness over everything in its path. Design and its offshoot branding were instrumental in stamping this uniformity on British high

Rick Poynor Talks about Writing Criticism

Founding editor, Eye *magazine*

If design can sometimes be too perfect or professionally crafted, can the same be said of writing?

It's hard to imagine an everyday writing situation where this could possibly be a problem. The more you revise and polish your writing, the better it tends to be. A point will come when the writing is good and is of a publishable standard, but even then it will improve if you continue to work on it. There is certainly a danger of overwriting and "purple prose," but neither of those traits is a sign of perfection or professionalism. The writing needs to achieve a balance of form and intent. If the rhetoric is faulty, through either overwriting or underwriting, then it won't convince. Writers should strive to do the best writing they can.

Do you tailor your voice to your audience?

The aim, naturally, is to maintain your voice. No ambitious writer wants to sound interchangeable with other writers, or to be squashed flat by a publication's unifying editorial style. Some people think they can only write in one way. They might be great geniuses but more probably they are just inflexible or inexperienced writers. Writers who aim to write for different outlets and audiences will need to make pragmatic adjustments to their style. Understanding what is possible within a particular context and saying what you want to say within those constraints are essential professional skills. Once you have mastered this, writing to suit different editorial formats is a pleasurable part of the craft.

What qualities do you think are common to the best design writing?

I'm not sure I want to distinguish here between design writing and ordinary writing. The qualities that make any writing good will also make design writing good. Depending on the genre of writing (report, essay, column, review, book chapter) these qualities might include a readable style, originality of language, clarity of expression, avoidance of cliché, precision of observation, accuracy of reporting, thoroughness of research, knowledge of the subject, the ability to tell a story, the ability to develop an argument, and a coherent personal point of view. Whatever the subject, the reader needs to feel that the writer has something valuable to say and that the writing is worth the time the reader puts in. The writing should be vital and fresh.

Do you have a typical research methodology?

I have regular ways of going about research, but these are so thoroughly ingrained now that I never think of them as a "research methodology." Reading is the most essential activity. I'm always scanning for information that relates to my existing interests and looking for new subjects to pursue in my writing. I did this before the Internet and now the Internet facilitates even wider-ranging searches. Nevertheless, my library of books, magazines, and journals, built up over many years and tailored to my present and

← Cover of the premier issue of *Eye* magazine, conceived and edited by Rick Poynor.

future research needs, remains my most essential research tool. I have filing cabinets full of cuttings dating back thirty years—and many more still to file. These printed materials are a constant reminder that a great deal of what you need to engage in historical research is not available online. Over the years, studio visits and recorded interviews have been crucial to my research. I still try to avoid email interviews when writing about someone. When necessary, I visit libraries and archives. A notebook is essential, of course, and increasingly I'm using my camera as an aide-mémoire and as way of generating visual material that might become the basis of an essay.

You've often discussed the difference between design criticism and journalism. How does this distinction manifest in your writing?

That's really a matter for the reader to decide. It's true that I have talked about the differences between criticism and journalism, and when I was working as an editor, I proposed "critical journalism" as a form of writing that might attempt to unite the positive aspects of both. I also tried to practice this myself. But I certainly never intended critical journalism to be a replacement for a purer kind of criticism. Critical journalism was a way of saying, "If we take a journalistic framework as our starting point—trade magazine, newspaper—is it possible to be more critical about design than standard practice usually allows?" I would like to see a design criticism aimed at the interested general reader that is independent of the academy (even if it's written by academics) and unconstrained by journalistic limitations. We see this approach in music and film writing—for instance, Continuum's 33 1/3 series and the BFI Film Classics series. It should also be possible in a popular subject like design. Yet there are still very few outlets.

There is no reason why criticism has to follow set paths. Analysis of the designed world can, and should, take visual forms.

streets to a degree that Nairn, who died in 1983, can scarcely have imagined. Many people find it harder to feel such a keen sense of outrage today because they have ceased to believe that it's likely to have much effect. What counts is to find ways of accommodating things as they are and of making whatever practical interventions you can lever, though these aren't expected to bring about fundamental change. In architectural circles, the term "post-critical" has gained currency as a way of describing some younger architects' acceptance of the prevailing social, economic and cultural reality. In a recent issue of *Harvard Design Magazine*, Reinhold Martin notes that this form of architecture is committed to "an affect-driven, nonoppositional, nonresistant, nondissenting and therefore nonutopian form of architectural production".

Reinhold wonders, with some justification, whether post-critical polemic might just be part of the general political swing to the right, an authoritarian manoeuvre intended to kill off once and for all any lingering traces in architectural thinking of the radical politics of the 1960s. If the post-critical position purports to be "realistic", then Reinhold proposes "utopian realism" as a riposte. "Utopian realism is critical," he writes. "It is real. It is enchantingly secular. It thinks differently. It is a style with no form. . . . It is utopian not because it dreams impossible dreams, but because it recognizes 'reality' itself as—precisely—an all-too-real dream enforced by those who prefer to accept a destructive and oppressive status quo." We are back to the idea that criticism's purpose is to strip away the layers and try to expose what is going on underneath. This task has nothing to do with professional and institutional needs to build careers and promote the design business.

So where does that leave the possibility of design criticism today? Britain has plenty of outlets for design journalism, but design criticism is much harder to find. The quickest way to

assess its state of health is to try naming some design critics, writers who are well known for consistent preoccupations and points of view, who are prepared to speak out and take a stand, and whose writing has a distinctive style and voice. If we use, say, the great Reyner Banham as a yardstick, is there anyone who measures up? Recently, I took part in two panel discussions about design criticism organised in London by *I.D.* magazine and Rhode Island School of Design. Part way through the second event I pointed out that no one on either panel had mentioned any design critics. I challenged my fellow panellist, *Icon's* editor Marcus Fairs, to name some—he proposed himself and his team. I threw in the name of Sam Jacob whose writing about design and popular culture in *Icon* and *Modern Painters* seems to me to display an individual voice. And that was it.

I would say we have a problem. We desperately need criticism. It's a vital part of the development of any creative discipline. It helps to shape the way practitioners think about their work and it plays a crucial role in fostering critical reflection among design students. Conducted convincingly, design criticism might even establish design in the public's consciousness—at last—as an activity that has a little more to it than dreaming up cool things to buy in the shops.

It comes back to our publications. The standard of design criticism is in the hands of the editors who commission most design writing. New writers cannot possibly emerge without places to publish and sympathetic support. The greatest gift an editor can give a writer is the space and freedom to explore a subject in a personal way; this was the opportunity that *AR* gave Nairn. Nurturing writers is a basic editorial task, but it's not clear that editors see it that way any more. Most magazine writing is publisher-led: this is what we need, this is our style, 1,200 words, go away and do it. What we see in the best blogs is a desire, in both writers and readers, for writing that shatters

⊘ₐ Andrea Lange Talks about Writing Criticism

Andrea Lange is the author of Writing About Architecture.

How does your writing style differ for online and print publications?

Not much. There are different formal conventions for online writing: You have to write to the jump, giving people a reason to click through after the first or second paragraph; you can write a list, whereas in print you might weave the list together with prose; you don't necessarily have to have a conclusion. That said, after writing for both for about two years, I don't even think about the differences anymore. I am more concerned with who it is for and how many words I have.

What place should sarcasm or snark have in design writing and criticism?

Snark is a loaded term. I think you can be sarcastic, mean, eviscerating, or whatever you want to call it as long as you aren't personal and as long as you back it up with facts (observation, example, visual data). Even if people disagree with your conclusions, they can tell you care enough to do your homework and aren't just being snarky to get attention.

Do you actively work to incite online discussion? If so, how?

I have found that the pieces that get the most comments are the ones that take the strongest position, and that encourages me to go out on a limb.

How do you deal with criticism of your writing?

I love getting edited, which happens infrequently these days. To have time to have a discussion with a smart, informed editor about making my writing better is a luxury. In terms of blog comments, I've been very lucky not to get a lot of snark. If people have a point, I try to respond either defending my position or acknowledging something I've overlooked. But most criticism I get is about content, not form.

Why is it important to include some salt in a sweet review?

If you are nothing but nice, it is not always clear that you are paying attention. Adding salt indicates that you have thought your rave through, and that you have equally good reasons for loving as well as hating. Nothing's perfect, and there's nothing more boring (to me) than bubbly enthusiasm.

What skills should one actively cultivate for critical design writing?

A clear head. I write quickly, primarily because I have already thought through my one point or three in my head for a couple of days before I need to start typing. Thinking things through helps you eliminate extras (if it is not important, you'll likely forget it) and hone in on the necessities. It balances first impressions and later ideas. It can take time to get in touch with what you really think; particularly if you are coming out of an environment, like school, where opinion is not necessarily emphasized. And it can take even more time to be able to write that opinion out succinctly. Blogs seem to offer the promise of thinking out loud, but if you are trying to write 500 words, that's not a lot of room to ruminate.

the chains imposed by narrow journalistic formats and agendas. If design magazines learn one lesson from blogs, it should be to put the emphasis back on good writing. Let's be utopian realists and ignore the old saw about designers not wanting to read. It isn't true. Publish commentary that is so timely, lively, perceptive, provocative, informative, irreverent and entertaining that people can't afford to miss it.

There is no reason why criticism has to follow set paths. Analysis of the designed world can, and should, take visual forms. The *AR* knew it 50 years ago. Yet it's surprising how rarely design magazines use the resources at their disposal— photographs, diagrams, illustrations—in partnership with words to deliver an incisive commentary on the visual realm. Why is the prevailing visual mode always celebratory? That might be appropriate for the glossy, weekend-break, luxury-lifestyle end of publishing, but not for magazines professing a commitment to design thinking. And why isn't humour used more often to puncture pretension and cut the over-mighty down to size? Music magazines have been doing this for years. While criticism needs space to stretch out, it can also be delivered in sharp, concentrated bursts. It should be as unpredictable and inventive as the best design.

❻ PUBLIC RELATIONS

When Sigmund Freud's nephew, Edward Bernays, ostensibly codified the American public relations profession in his book *Propaganda* (1928), he developed a theater of persuasion and a language that all the actors would share.

Publicity writing is different from most any other form of writing. The intent is clearly to manipulate points of view and create greater awareness of a product or idea. Sometimes PR is simply the facts, other times it is couching those facts in a favorable context. In all cases it serves to direct the reader toward a portal of some kind.

There is an art to PR, which most neophytes don't quite understand how to achieve. It is not the same as journalism, although often the same tropes for capturing attention are used. Here is part of a press release that was used to announce a film festival I worked on in 2012. Originally, I thought it would be best to start with a jolt:

Is the book dead? Will it become a cultural relic like vinyl LPs and rotary telephone phones? Do you know the history of Levi's 501 Jeans or the Barcelona chair?

But the above approach was probably better written as advertising copy (an entirely different discipline), not a press release that strives to be informational without too much hype. The Communications Office wrote this calmer alternative:

School of Visual Arts presents the SVA/BBC Design Film Festival featuring a once-in-a lifetime chance to view groundbreaking BBC films that have never previously been screened in the United States.

The program includes design, advertising, and book-related films on topics such as the future of the book, the history of Levi's 501 Jeans and the Barcelona chair, and real-life stories of the ad men—and women—behind the fictional television series Mad Men. *Curated by Steven Heller, co-chair of the MFA Design Department at SVA, and Adam Harrison Levy, faculty member in the MFA Design Criticism Department at SVA, the festival takes place Saturday, March 24, 1 – 9pm, at the SVA Theatre, 333 West 23 Street. The festival marks the New York premiere of* The Book: the Last Chapter?, *an inventive and thought-provoking documentary about the fate of the book in the age of the iPad and the Kindle. Writers including Gary Shteyngart and Douglas Coupland, publishing entrepreneurs and literary agents, weigh in on this crucial cultural question.*

In the final analysis, a less demonstrative or aggressive approach was preferred. All the essential information was presented up front and the receiver got the entire story without being assaulted. I asked Michael Grant, who directs public relations at the School of Visual Arts, to explain the art and craft of PR writing.

Q/A Michael Grant Talks about Effective Publicity

Michael Grant is director of communications at the School of Visual Arts, New York.

What constitutes effective public relations/corporate communications?

As a professional communicator, your goal is always twofold: to strengthen your relationships with your supporters, and to enlist new ones. In both cases, you start with shared interests. There are many different yardsticks for success that one can use (newspaper circulation numbers, clicks, tweets, subscribers, etc.), but I like to think of the process as a dinner party. If you manage to catch up with an old friend, make an introduction, and meet someone new, you're doing well. That may sound simplistic, but when it comes to communicating with a large and ever-changing community—even one as well respected as the School of Visual Arts, where I work—it's helpful. We're looking for opportunities to be the dinner party's host: whether it's in the New York Times, on Facebook or Tumblr, or at a venue that hasn't even been built yet.

What are the three main characteristics in writing a public relations announcement?

The answer depends somewhat on the occasion. When it comes to the textbook press release (yes, there still is a place in this world for the press release), there are certain "golden rules" that apply to the format, tone, and organization of content. In my experience they apply to design announcements as they do in other areas. Make it as easy to scan as possible (respect the journalist's time), be as objective as you can (respect the journalist's intelligence), and provide as much relevant and accurate information as you can (respect the journalist's need for reliable content). I'm only doing my job if an announcement answers a simple question: What's at stake for the intended audience? In other words, what does the reader stand to gain, what's he or she being asked to do, and why act now?

In writing these blog items, what is your goal?

At its foundation, the work we do is storytelling. We want to tell stories that readers, in turn, tell their friends, coworkers, and families. With social media, we can observe the process in real time, as people share, comment, or "like" content. When it comes to writing about design, we're interested in stories that are not just shared by designers or people in the business. We're thinking of the parent of a nondesign student, the sculptor who is a fine arts alumnus, and the magazine culture editor. We want to demonstrate the ubiquity of design, the power of the designer, and the role that SVA faculty, students, and alumni can play in changing the world.

Is there any room for "personal style" in blog items like these?

Yes, and where personal style comes through is in the tone and emphasis. Blogging can be more conversational and colloquial than writing for print or traditional reporting, which is a big part of its appeal. On the SVA blog, for example, we use multiple contributors and don't credit our writers (or

disclose personal information), but the reader should still feel like there's a human being on the other end, someone who's interested in the subject at hand. All blogging comes down to "Hey look!" whether it's more news or feature-oriented, and a personal voice can go a long way. The real question is whether or not anyone will go back and read this stuff years from now—if it can even be found at that point.

What is the difference between these blog items and a press release?

Blogging is originally a vehicle for opinion, and it's a rapid-release, short-acting dose. The format is reactive—you're often piggy-backing on other news—in getting your message out. And the blogging platform makes it possible to offer up lots of visuals and multimedia, so the copy becomes less important. A press release is a news vehicle, and is meant to provide journalists with a factual basis for reporting. Blogs and releases are both forms of endorsement, but the stakes are different. A release needs to justify the extra time involved in unpacking it because it's a claim to vgetting on the public record.

Is there a formula for getting a press release noticed?

I wish there were! The simple answer is, know who you're sending a release to, and why, before you even start writing. PR folks like to say we're writing releases that are ready to publish, and there's some truth to that. If you can't imagine a release appearing—maybe just in part—in the target outlet, you need to start over. The headline and deck of a release should also pass a basic test for newsworthiness and timeliness: Why does the world need this information now? As the media landscape has evolved, and journalists have more demands on their time, there's greater impatience and suspicion toward press releases. If you can't attach a personal message to a release, you're not likely to get serious attention.

Are there any dos or don'ts on writing for the press?

Like all relationships, the interaction we have with journalists is specific to the individuals involved—and timing plays a big part in generating publicity. Members of the press expect PR professionals to do their homework, and rightly so. They're often inundated by pitches and press releases. Don't assume any background knowledge on the reporter's part (you should be prepared to write the story you're pitching), but do consider how you communicate. Some reporters want to be pitched on Twitter any time of day or night. Some people want to receive a fax at their office between the hours of 4 and 5 p.m. Finally, a good litmus test for press outreach is, "Would I want to open this 400th email of the day?"

 BLOG

Exclusive online writing, particularly for weblogs, must not be ignored (although sometimes I'd like to ignore it). The blog has become a breeding ground for many fine writers and thinkers, and a bottomless well of unique information and ideas. An increasingly growing number of readers are getting their nourishment from blogs, often in bite-size servings.

Blogs are happier when the short form is used. But the long form is also present within these precincts. Routinely the blog style is more informal (sometimes only lightly edited, if at all), but the quick and loose approach appeals to the reader who has limited time and lots to digest.

There is also a tendency to write in the first person, with many asides, winks, and nods. When done judiciously, this adds to the enjoyment of the read. When overdone, well, it is like fingernails scratching a blackboard.

Blog topics range from obscure to newsworthy, ultra-ephemeral to highly intellectual, arcane rants and raves to intensely researched essays. But the main virtue is immediacy: capturing the zeitgeist in comparatively short bites. There is sometimes virtuosity in those captures.

Blogs give everyone a virtual printing press, and that's good. What is bad is that it gives anyone an often unmediated soapbox. We still have the option of engaging or not, but blogs are part of the daily conversation. Blogs are quoted; bloggers are taken seriously; blog reports have sometimes even influenced daily news and public policy.

The range of concern and the level of quality were all over the lot. The blogosphere is composed of a slew of individual blogs. Some are indeed logs or diaries that reveal personal interests and quirks; others are ersatz journals that offer serious points of view. In the design world there are a handful of well-visited blogs, but I was surprised to find so many design-related or design-interested blogs where aficionados are holding forth either too many or too few. Whether blogs will evolve into other writing genres is left to be seen, but for now, they are significant outlets for information, expression, and more.

The remainder of this section includes several different types of blogs. Gail Anderson's blog post on *Print* magazine's Imprint website addresses her teaching experience and exemplifies a breezy style that is characteristic of blog writing. Similarly, Liz Danzico's post on online etiquette is a story that might not have found a publishing home if not for the accessibility of personal blogs. The personal blog allows the blogger an opportunity to try out different styles and voices. Graphic designer Sean Adams uses his blog to share insights in a personal manner.

CASE STUDY:
SCHOOL DAYS

GAIL ANDERSON

Gail Anderson is a designer and professor at the School of Visual Arts, New York.
(Originally published November 16, 2011 on Imprint, *http://imprint.printmag.com/design-school/school-days/)*

After 20-plus years as adjunct faculty at the School of Visual Arts, I still get myself all knotted up at the beginning of each semester. Will everyone drop the class? Will they see me for the fraud that I am? Standard issue concerns. And perhaps I was even more nervous this September, since for the first time I was taking on a full course load as part of my plan to reinvent myself. I was thinking *Room 222*, but was afraid I'd end up with *Welcome Back, Kotter*.

I started teaching while I was still in my twenties, and wasn't much older than the continuing ed students in my first class. I arrived for the initial session in the middle of a torrential downpour, soaking wet, portfolio wrapped in a black garbage bag. I nervously asked if I was in the right room, and am guessing the students probably hoped I wasn't.

I quickly learned that teaching required the ability to clearly articulate a point of view. You couldn't just tell a student that their project "didn't work." You had to be able to tell them WHY a piece didn't work, and suggest ways to make it better. It was paramount to both instill confidence and challenge the students, which could be a tenuous balance when there was little to be salvaged, or, frankly, if I was in a lousy mood.

I was surprised that I was able to string coherent thoughts together and then repeat them out loud, and that people took me somewhat seriously. Teaching was a good dress rehearsal for dealing with editors and clients, and it forced me to speak up and not fade into the background. I liked the continuing ed students, and they seemed to like me. I was hooked.

SVA has become home to a much larger population of international students than in the olden days when I was commuting down from my parents' house in the Bronx, or living at Sloane House, the very first SVA dorm, a slightly sad YMCA on West 34th Street. I don't remember any international students in my Foundation Year group, and thought we were exotic because we hailed from all five boroughs, Long Island, New Jersey, and even Connecticut. We were decidedly local

↑ *The ABC's of Being a Twin* by Kelly Shami

*Teaching keeps you young, exposes you to cultural references
that you may never know about otherwise...*

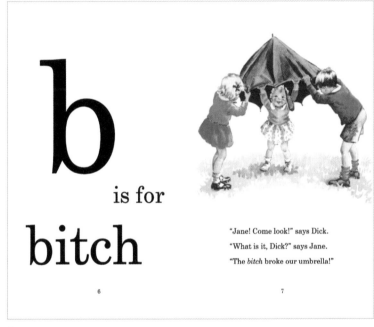

↑ *The ABC's of Cussing* by Jennifer Sims

↑ *The ABC's of What's for Dinner* by Lauren Hom

and mostly came from neighborhoods with adjoining houses. Today's SVA students are far more worldly, and with each new class, I end up meeting students from truly exotic places (and I say this with all due respect to my beloved boroughs and tri-state area).

Working with diverse groups hailing from so many countries can be difficult at first. Other cultures sometimes teach their students to defer to instructors, which is diametrically opposed to the way American students are taught to behave. And we blustery New Yorkers can be much more assertive than even our Midwestern peers.

Language can be a delicate issue, as are American pop culture references, and I give students who've come to the States all alone kudos for extreme bravery. I only ventured from the Bronx to Manhattan and the two worlds could not have been more different. Assimilating into a whole new culture shows a level of maturity that is to be acknowledged, particularly when there isn't even a distant cousin or cat-loving aunt anywhere nearby.

Teaching a worldlier crowd has also been kind of a kick, since I've gotten to know a little about life on the other side of the country, as well as the other side of the globe. I have a fabulous third-year student named Zipeng, who cocks his head and teases me with, "What IS that?" when I make a dumb pop culture reference—particularly about anything that dates further back than his short lifetime. Zipeng is a real live wire, and I suddenly find myself wanting to go to China, his homeland. I've met Turkish students who were ridiculously talented, including a few teenagers who came over to participate in the SVA Pre-College program last summer. I'm

now ready to go to Turkey when I get back from China. I've worked with tons of gifted Korean students, folks from Saudi Arabia, Israel, Russia, Japan, Spain, Indonesia, Cambodia, and even a few countries I had to sheepishly Google.

If you've never taught, I say go for it. Teaching keeps you young, exposes you to cultural references that you may never know about otherwise, and students are always up on the best websites and music. You'll look smarter in front of your own kids, nieces, or nephews. And you'll know who someone named Florence and the Machine is.

❶ *Zipeng Zhu*, from my 2011–2012 Communication in Graphic Design third year class.

❷ *ABC's of a Sassy Little Asian Girl* by Jessie Gang

❸ *The ABC's of Chinglish* by Zipeng Zhu

❹ *The ABC's of Drug Slang* by Melanie Chernock

❺ *The ABC's of Awkward Situations* by Sandra Woodruff

CASE STUDY:

"THANK YOU," OR WHY SOCRATES WAS WRONG

LIZ DANZICO

Liz Danzico is the chair of MFA Interaction Design at the School of Visual Arts, New York.
(Originally published October 19, 2009 on Bobulate, *http://bobulate.com/post/205253518/on-thank-you-or-why-socrates-was-wrong)*

As she drove us home in the blue Fiat that first week of fourth grade, my mother began by announcing that it was time for me to begin writing thank you notes.

"When you've received a present (referring to my new tennis racket), you must follow up by saying thanks with a card or a letter," she instructed. "It's good manners." So there I was. Torn between manners and a racket. Upon arriving home, she introduced me to Emily Post.

While the merits of Emily Post are much contested, the sentiment had the right intention. The formula is quite simple: when someone does something for you, say thank you.

It was an invaluable piece of advice that I've followed in my adult life, writing thank you notes for all things—big, small, monumental, and frivolous. And always within 48 hours of the happening. All very personal. Never a Hallmark. Never a pre-printed affair. Never the same twice. Always something I have to dash off myself.

But there is some finesse to writing the thank you. Or at least a handful of things to keep in mind. Here are my guidelines to writing the critical note:

Thank you notes are tangible notes whenever possible.

These notes are all done by hand whenever possible, sent via USPS mail. A follow-up-thank-you (a thank-you for a gesture on a second occasion) may be done via email, SMS, DM, Facebook, or whatever your choice of media; regardless, the text should be composed with care.

Thank you notes need not be "notes."

Write your thank you notes on other objects. Second to notes, I send thank-you books quite often, writing the note of gratitude inside. Thank-you videos are time-intensive, but family members receive them. Newsprint, photos, negatives. There are choices.

You want busy people to read your thank you note too.

Thus, keep it short; do not restate the obvious; and give busy people something of value to read. Personal contacts and good information they aren't aware of count as value. Don't ask busy people for more. (And, of course, under no circumstances, ever, should you write out a URL by hand in a thank you note.)

Set up a thank-you framework.

The biggest obstacle to thanking is sometimes the tools. Phone, email, letter, SMS—options get in the way. Do yourself a favor and set up a thank-you framework. Get some cards, stamps, or even an email template. Do not send one-word emails of "thanks."

Thanks.

Much later on than fourth grade, I was quite troubled to read Socrates urging that "writing destroys memory." His intention, of course, was that those who use writing will become forgetful, relying on external resources for what they lack. I think these written transcriptions over a past event don't destroy memory, but might, in fact, preserve it. Clearly, Socrates had just never received a thank you note.

CASE STUDY:
ART NOUVEAU FEEDER FETISHIST

⮞ **SEAN ADAMS**

Sean Adams is a partner at AdamsMorioka.
(Originally published February 21, 2012 on Burning Settlers Cabin, *www.burningsettlerscabin.com/?p=7487)*

What I want to talk about here is fat. Not "phat" fat, but "fat" fat. Everyone is concerned about the country getting fatter. But what happened to typography and shapes in the late 1960s and 1970s? They got fat.

I understand the issue of anti-consumerism. Coming from an anti-establishment counterculture environment in the 1960s, companies needed to make messages and products "big." Bigger was better, and if it could also be in earth colors and look natural, even better. If I actually purchased an item, rather than making it on my loom at home with macramé, I wanted to know I was getting my money's worth. So we see fat logos, wide lapels and ties, big shirt collars, bell bottoms, and giant brown cars.

I am ashamed to admit this, but I like fat Victorian shapes. It's as if the Garamond and curly shapes ate too many French fries and went from delicate to, well, very, very healthy. All the years of praising refined letterforms and deriding bold serifs have led to this shameful admission. Granted, in the hands of a master such as Herb Lubalin or Tom Carnase, the results are spectacular. But, when abused by someone less adroit, the result is clunky, horsey, and [vomitus] (yes this is now a word when discussing ugly typography). I hope this post will prove my veracity and commitment to the truth. We only tell the truth here, at any cost. This admission will, no doubt, ruin any chances of ever receiving an AIGA medal, being invited to join AGI, or being spoken to by any of my friends. So be kind when

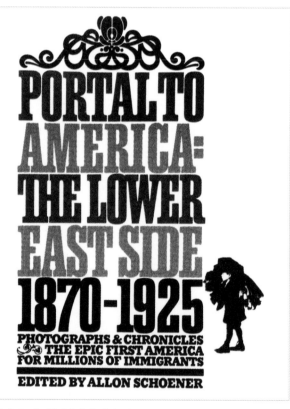

↑ Book design by Herb Lubalin belends Art Nouveau into a contemporary context.

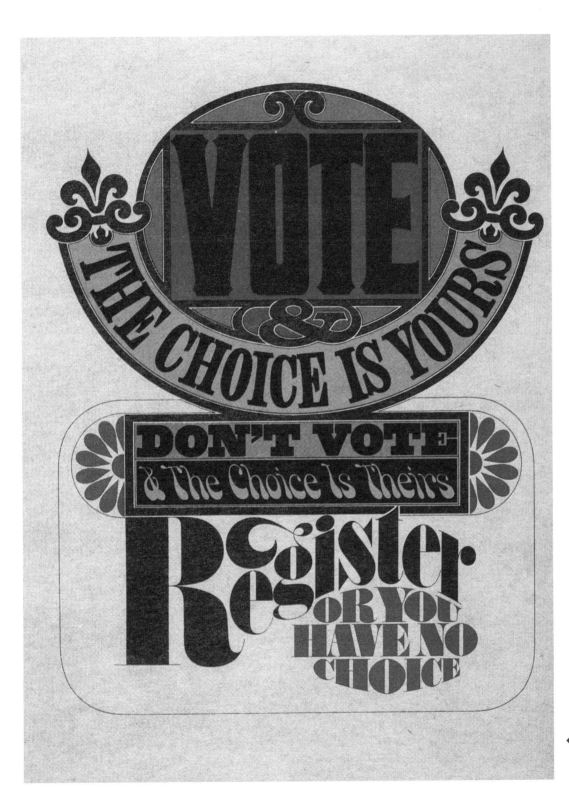

← *Poster design* by
Herb Lubalin uses
Victorian letterforms
in a new fashion.

you find me at a conference sitting alone as other designers point and whisper, "Oh, yes, it's true. He has a secret thing for the chunky type."

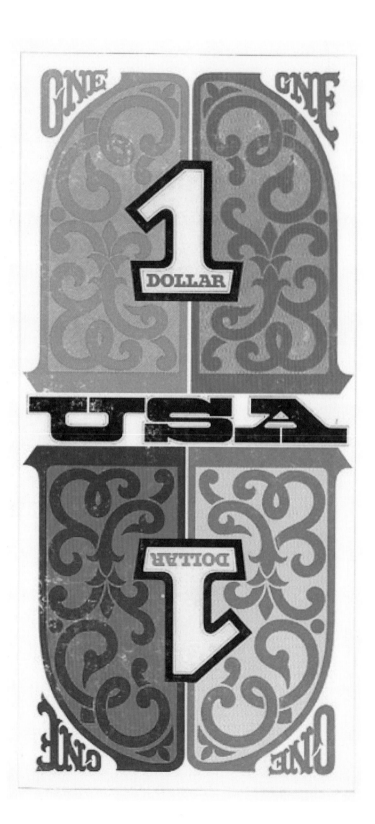

Lubalin was neither modern nor post-modern, he typifies the ecclectic approach to graphic design, with a nod toward the decorative in past styles from Victorian and Art Nouveau preiods. Here are some that he and other designers created under his art direction.

Sean Adams Talks about Blogging

Partner, Adams Morioka

Your blog posts on BurningSettlersCabin.com are often under 300 words. Why?

Simply, people don't read long posts. If I need deep information, I'll go to *Design Observer*. I consider *Burning Settlers Cabin* the easy-read version of *DO*. I also have a full-time job and teach, so I don't have time for 2,500-word posts.

How many times do you rewrite your blog posts?

Rarely. I might go back and fix a grammatical or spelling issue, but the posts are closer to stream of consciousness than actual writing (as you can plainly read). The point of the blog was to provide me an opportunity to talk about things that interest me and state my personal opinion. If someone dislikes a post or disagrees with a political stance, that post will be replaced with another one within a day or two. I find it works best for me to not overthink or overwrite a post.

What triggers a blog idea?

I'd like to say that I scour the library, or drive through Los Angeles searching for interesting ideas. But that would be a lie. If my brain were to be scanned, I believe it would prove that I have a giant iPhoto album in place of cognitive processes. The blog gives me a chance to do something when my mind is stuck in a Saul Bass, Hawaii 5-0, or Tomorrowland cycle. I do my best to rotate the themes such as graphic design, film, or history on a daily basis. This helps to focus the idea. Today is a film day; I'll talk about *A Summer Place*. The issue for me is not a lack of ideas, but a surplus of bad ideas.

Your posts are always in the first person. Have you every written in the second or third?

No, that would be like having a conversation and using the third person when discussing myself. The blog is my voice. As stated on DVDs, the opinions stated do not reflect the view of the management. As I am not God and omniscient, first person is appropriate when I am yammering on about my views.

What is the most satisfying part of blogging?

I don't approach the blog concerned about increasing readership. If I did that, I would end up posting innocuous ideas that wouldn't offend anyone, just like network sitcoms. It gives me a venue to talk about anything I want and say whatever I believe. That sounds like the basis of good democracy.

Burning Settlers Cabin
Good and Plain Optimism from AdamsMorioka

Art-Nouveau Feeder Fetishist

From bare-breasted Indian maidens on earliest handbills to present day catchphrases such as "Should a gentleman offer a Tiparillo to a lady?", sex has always been used to sell tobacco. For psychologists, the connection between smoking and sex is as obvious as a nipple on a breast. Smoking has its roots in the oral erotic pleasure derived from infantile sucking and so does much of sex play. Nineteenth Century tobacco advertising linked sex and tobacco perhaps more beautifully (and naively) than any advertising before or since. It is from that period that we present the cigar box labels on the following eight pages.

Herb Lubalin

Search

Links
» AdamsMorioka
» AIGA
» Art Center College of Design
» Cathy of California
» DaveLand
» Design Observer
» Felt and Wire
» How
» Imagineering Disney
» Library of Congress PPOC
» Mohawk Fine Papers
» Passport to Dreams Old & New
» Retro Renovation
» Under Consideration
» Virginia Historical Society

Meta
» Site Admin
» Log out
» Entries RSS
» Comments RSS
» WordPress.org

Recent Posts
» I was a Teenage Teenager
» Deep Impact
» How to Have Fun
» Musings of the Mad
» Art-Nouveau Feeder Fetishist

Archives
» March 2012
» February 2012
» January 2012
» December 2011
» November 2011
» October 2011
» September 2011
» August 2011
» July 2011

What I want to talk about here is fat. Not "phat" fat, but fat fat. Everyone is concerned about the country getting fatter. But what happened to typography and shapes in the late 1960s and 1970s? They got fat. I understand the issue of anti-consumerism. Coming from an anti-establishment counter-culture environment in the 1960s, companies needed to make messages and products "big." Bigger was better, and if it could also be in earth colors and look natural, even better. If I actually purchased an item, rather than making it on my loom at home with macramé, I wanted to know I was getting my money's worth. So we see fat logos, wide lapels and ties, big shirt collars, bell bottoms, and giant brown cars.

I am ashamed to admit this, but I like fat Victorian shapes. It's as if the Garamond and curly shapes ate too many French fries and went from delicate to, well, very, very healthy. All the years of praising refined letterforms and deriding bold serifs have led to this shameful admission. Granted, in the hands of a master such as Herb Lubalin or Tom Carnase, the results are spectacular. But, when abused by someone less adroit, the result is clunky, horsey, and vomitous (yes this is now a word when discussing ugly typography). I hope this post will prove my veracity and commitment to the truth. We only tell the truth here, at any cost. This admission will, no doubt, ruin any chances of ever receiving an AIGA medal, being invited to join AGI, or being spoken to by any of my friends. So be kind when you find me at a conference sitting alone as other designers point and whisper, "Oh, yes, it's true. He has a secret thing for the chunky type."

RAY BARBER

In writing his *Burning Settlers Cabin* blog, Sean Adams locates informational and ecclectic visuals to illustrate his routinely short posts.

… there's nothing better than hitting Publish, dropping the link onto Facebook and Twitter, and watching the story find its way into the world.

Q/A Alissa Walker Talks about Her Favorite Form of Writing

Alissa Walker is a writer and USC Annenberg Getty Arts Journalism Fellow.

Why do you blog?

I blog for three reasons: one, to work through and test out theories or concepts that I'm wrestling with in my "official" stories ("official" meaning the ones I get paid to write); two, I use my blog as a way to promote events and other real-life happenings that I'm either speaking at or helping to organize; three, I write to share little snippets of the world that I encounter and I want to pass along because they're beautiful, or funny, or poignant, or weird. There's definitely plenty of weird on my blog.

Do you prefer blogging to other forms of writing?

Besides tweeting, if you can count that as a form of writing, it's absolutely my favorite. There are many (many) merits to writing for print publications, of course. But there's nothing better than hitting Publish, dropping the link onto Facebook and Twitter, and watching the story find its way into the world. I love the instant reaction I get from my readers, and how they express delight or disappointment for my story. And I love watching the trail it leaves as it gets passed along from one person to another. It's pretty amazing that writers can track all that now.

Why do you call your blog *A Walker in LA*?

Believe it or not, my blog has been recently renamed. I started it with the name *Gelatobaby* when I launched it, which was supposed to serve as a reminder of an incredible trip to Italy that jumpstarted my writing career. But over the years I went through many personal changes: getting rid of my car, walking more, shifting toward being interested in cities and transportation—and all of those found their way onto the blog. In a way, the blog opened up a whole new world of writing for me. So I wanted to come up with a new name that fit the writer I am today. Plus, since my last name is Walker, I now have some powerful brand synergy!

What prompts an idea for *A Walker in LA*?

I started my blog to explore ideas that I didn't get paid to write. Most often, a post comes from something I see on the streets while walking in Los Angeles. What usually happens is I see something out in the urban environment, snap a photo with my iPhone, come home, and stare at the photo and wonder, "Now, why is that?"

Does your approach to writing change in the blog format?

I have a special blog voice that is far more accessible and conversational (and dare I say funny?) than my other writings. I feel like I can really be myself on my own blog. I can play around with language, I can make inappropriate jokes—I can take risks here because it's my place.

Do you believe the blog form will lead to something else?

So many people are already saying that the blog is dead; that Tumblr and Twitter and whatever else have killed it. But I don't see blogging going anywhere. I still stumble across the most wonderful stories by writers I've never heard of before. What I'd like to see is a system for paying for great stories, maybe like Amazon's Kindle Single program or like iTunes, where you could sell your best work for a dollar. I'd like to be able to make money on my own blogging, but I feel like selling advertising isn't right for me.

Rainbow bright
Posted on June 8, 2012 by Alissa

love and highly recommend riding LA's transit system, here's how i do it.

Climb some stairs
Join me and some of LA's most interesting people for The Big Parade, an annual 40-mile walk through Los Angeles over the city's many public stairways. Read about this year's walk, or come along for a practice walk (sometimes hosted by me), which take place throughout the year.

Listen to DnA: Design and Architecture
Tune in to DnA: Design & Architecture, the KCRW show hosted by Frances Anderton on the third Tuesday of every month, where I'm an associate producer. For local design events, check out the DnA calendar.

Bring GOOD ideas for Cities to your city or school
An initiative funded in part by ArtPlace, GOOD ideas for Cities asks creatives to create solutions to urban problems proposed by city leaders, and present the results at lively public forums. Read more about this program I co-founded with GOOD's Casey Caplowe and CEOs for Cities Julia Kleiner, and

A few weeks ago I traveled to a magical place in the desert with 22 of my closest girlfriends.

THE
EDITORIAL
ROLE

IDEA

The editor is essential to any kind of writing. She is originator, mediator, and facilitator. She is keeper of old standards and developer of new ones. She is the first and last one to read your manuscript.

One pair of eyes on text is simply not enough. Too many mistakes—man-made or machine-made—can occur all too easily. If there is one piece of advice to heed it is this: Reread, reread, reread. Then have someone else reread it too. And all this, if possible, before it goes to the editor. Granted, this is not always possible, but it is the ideal.

Editors have other essential duties. They are sounding boards for ideas (often shooting down the bad ones) and developers of story concepts. They are architects of narratives (restructuring when necessary) and archaeologists too (often finding the buried lead stuck in the third paragraph). They are repositories of technical and ephemeral knowledge that you may or may not have but can always tap into during the course of a writing project. Editors can save you embarrassment when they catch the inevitable errors.

Since many designers are first-time writers, the editor is also the guide through what could seem like a complex process. I have asked some respected editors to shed light on their roles and methods.

ℚ⁄ₐ Sue Apfelbaum Talks about What an Editor Does

Former managing editor of AIGA Journal

What is the role of an editor?

An editor identifies a content need and works with an author to deliver writing that fulfills that expectation, ensuring that it communicates effectively with equal consideration for the author, publisher, and audience.

An editor helps make an author read better. Doesn't that make the editor an author?

No. In the same way that a coach can help an athlete to excel or a director can elicit a moving performance from an actor, an editor works to bring out the best in a writer so that the article or book, or whatever form the content might take, is as clear and engaging as can be. Editors can also be strong writers, but they aren't necessarily the subject experts that their writers are. Editors need writers, and writers need editors. Neither is as good without the other.

How far should an editor go in changing text?

There's no hard-and-fast rule here, but editors should absolutely make sure that their authors are aware (and consenting) of any radical revisions from the original draft. In the case of copywriting, an editor can take more liberties, but if a published work carries an author's byline, an editor should make sure the text is still true to the author's intent.

Should an editor always have an ear for the authorial voice?

For journalists it's more important to deliver a factual and balanced story than to interject a personal voice; a news editor would be justified in making the voice more neutral. In criticism and other types of editorial writing, the author's voice is imperative and should be considered a valuable attribute of the writing. A good editor recognizes what the author is trying to say and helps her to say it in a way that benefits both author and reader.

What is the most common problem faced by a writer who is writing about design?

Perhaps one obstacle to design writing is public awareness of what design actually is. The writer might need to help the reader to see things that might have gone unnoticed before. But the challenge of writing about design is the challenge of writing about anything.

Many designers are visual thinkers who struggle when it comes to articulating their ideas in writing. Maybe writing hasn't come to them as naturally as drawing or other forms of expression. Like anything worth doing, writing requires practice and discipline. No one gets it right the first time, not even writers. Just as designers revise and redo their work, writers draft and redraft. So, perhaps for designers, the first challenge is to get over any preconceptions that "I'm just not good at writing." Designers do user testing to improve their work and ensure its effectiveness. And writers need to have others read what they've written to know if they're making any sense.

Is there a trick to writing about design that is unique to this form?

The only trick to writing well is to resolve the question of, Am I making sense? Will anyone else understand what I want them to take away from my words? The only way to know is to let people read it and give you their feedback.

To write anything that's worth reading is a challenge, whether your subject is design or a piece of music or what you had for dinner last night. In each instance, you might start out thinking, "I don't know enough about <blank> to be writing about this." But of course you do. You don't have to position yourself as the world's foremost authority on the subject; you just have to be able to say something that's unique to your experience with it. Perhaps start by thinking about who created it, what they created and who it was created for, and if you consider it successful (if not, then why). Compare it to other design work (or music or meals) you've experienced. It can be hard to find the right words. But just as you learn more about design through exposure to it, you can improve as a writer simply by reading more writing.

What is your definition of a good piece of writing?

Good writing doesn't make me feel stupid. It doesn't make me have to stop and reread it to see if I missed something along the way, or have to look up words or lingo that I haven't heard before. Good writing, in the end, makes me feel smarter, like I've learned something. It might inspire me to have a conversation with someone about it or make me curious enough to want to read more on that subject or by that author. For me it feels as though a door has been opened and now I'm free to explore what lies ahead.

A good editor recognizes what the author is trying to say and helps her to say it in a way that benefits both author and reader.

Q/A Aaron Kenedi Talks about Editing a Design Magazine

Former Editor-in-Chief, Print *Magazine*

How did you become an editor?

Truthfully, I realized I wasn't a good enough designer or a dedicated enough writer to make it in either of those areas alone, but I was pretty good at them both. I had a decent sense of each discipline and the people who worked in them, so editor of a design magazine turned out to be the perfect job to combine my experience and skills in both areas.

What is the primary difference between editing in general and editing for a design publication?

The design community (especially in New York) is a very particular, passionate, and outspoken group, so to edit for them you really have to possess a few key attributes: knowledge of the industry and the key members; a point of view and opinion that you're willing to stand behind; and a willingness to take chances. Plus, of course, as a design magazine a lot of what we feature is imagery, so sometimes we have to let the imagery do the talking and edit out the text altogether. Knowing when and how to do that is a challenge.

What do you look for in a writer: Good ideas? Good writing style?

First I look for someone who can approach an idea in a new way. There are a lot of stories out there due to the constant media cycle we live in, but that's given over to a kind of accepted laziness that I think has tarnished the journalism profession. Next I look for level of commitment and devotion to researching a story that entails more than just a simple Google search. Then I look at his or her reporting approach (are they talking to the right people, are they staying on theme of both the story and the magazine, are they organized, etc.). Then, and this is really important, can they deliver on time? Someone who does all that gets hired.

Do you believe that a good editor can make a mediocre writer much better?

Yes.

What qualities do you look for in a publishable article?

A unique angle on a topic goes a long way. Always I look for whether the idea would interest me if I were a reader, which I am. And then I look at writing skill. I also personally like a lot of quotes and sidebar type of info, to give some personality and varying perspective to the piece. Hopefully a reader will read every word of the article, but if they just skimmed and looked at headlines, quotes, and captions they should still get more than just a gist.

Print, February 2012

What don't you want to see in a manuscript?

Laziness and sloppiness. Sparse or missing quotes. Overlooked or ignored angles. Erroneous assumptions. Bad storytelling.

What makes you happy as an editor?

Clarity. Good storytelling. An effective combination of words and images to create a satisfying story. And, of course, someone who can execute a pitch effectively and on time.

What makes you frustrated?

I see mistakes or missed opportunities that we could have gotten right the first time with enough time and focus. Or a really excited author who pitches a great idea and then can't deliver. That really drives me nuts.

When working with a new writer is there a process that's different from working with a more experienced one?

Often with new writers the biggest hurdle is just getting them familiar with the tone of a publication. And that's a very important role an editor can play. Even with a very good writer, sometimes the angle or the mood can take a while to get down (and sometimes the editors don't even know it themselves; then you have a big problem).

There are a lot of stories out there due to the constant media cycle we live in, but that's given over to a kind of accepted laziness that I think has tarnished the journalisim profession.

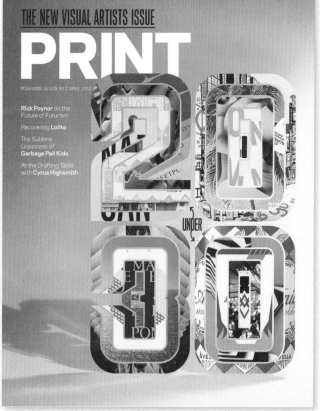

Aaron Kenedi's Favorite *Print* Spreads

SPREAD ❶ I thought this was a really nice piece of profile writing about an artist who not a lot of people have heard of, but has had a considerable impact on the New York art scene. It's told with a nice balance of reverence, affection, and information. Plus, I love the color scheme of the photo and the cropping that features her hands. A nice package all around.

SPREAD ❷ I love this spread, less for the writing than for the sheer information organization and delivery. It's probably one of the most intricate graphics we've ever run, and even though it's extremely busy, the information is presented in such a clear way that you have no trouble figuring out the main message and the connections of each designer.

SPREAD ❸ This is the first story I assigned as editor-in-chief of *Print*, and it was somewhat of an ambitious topic for us. I really wanted to focus on design as something bigger and broader than just ink on paper or products or websites. I wanted to display it as the thread that weaves myriad disciplines together. Showcasing baseball player Tim Lincecum's pitching motion as a designed thing was just too good to pass up, especially for the "Movement" issue. Angela Riechers' writing is superb here; she keeps the focus on Lincecum but manages to connect all the right design dots, so the reader never feels like the topic is a stretch for *Print* magazine. And the graphics are perfect as well. Probably my favorite story package so far at *Print*.

SPREAD ❹ I admit I chose this one more for its visual impact than its writing.

SPREAD ❺ This is just a fun piece for me. I love the contrast between the serious and technical writing of Paul Shaw and the whimsical commentary of Stephen Coles. This is a fairly new column and the writers haven't quite hit their stride in working together, so when we got the first draft, Paul had written so much copy that Stephen didn't have anywhere to play. So, instead of featuring just one of them, which we didn't want to do (the department is called "Stereotype" after all), we had the idea that Stephen would comment on Paul's thoughts. We didn't realize it would be so funny and lighthearted, but it is and I think it works really well.

Spread ❶: *Print*, December 2010; Photo: Henrik Knudsen

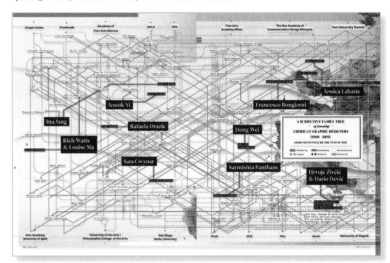

Spread ❷ March/April 2011; Design: Michael Worthington and Yasmin Khan of LA studio Counterspace

Spread ❸: August 2011; Design: Spin.

Spread ❹: August 2011; Design: Spin

Ruder's Univers
Weingart's Akzidenz
Vignelli's Haas
Brodovitch's Didone

Univers LT Std 65 Bold
Berthold Akzidenz Grotesk Bold
Commercial Type Haas Grot Text Bold
HdtF Didot 24 Medium

By **Paul Shaw** and Stephen Coles

WE ARE ACCUSTOMED today to typefaces as an element of a business or institutional identity. Often, it is the only one, usurping the prominent role once played by the logo. But there is a flip side to this: designers who are identified by the typefaces they use. This is especially true of designers who came of age in the pre-DTP days. These designers had a much smaller range of typefaces than there are today, and that range was further restricted by the fact that most were proprietary to one typesetting system or another.

Thus, we find a designer such as Reid Miles repeatedly using the same handful of typefaces in his famous Blue Note album covers. Executed between 1956 and 1967, the covers employ Caslon 540, Bodoni, Century, Craw Clarendon, News Gothic, Franklin Gothic, and Alternate Gothic over and over again. What these typefaces have in common is that they are all foundry type from American Type Founders. There are no European typefaces such as Times Roman, Palatino, Univers, Akzidenz Grotesk, or even Futura on Miles's covers. He worked with what was readily at hand.

With only a few good typefaces available, designers often made choices that they then clung to for the rest of their careers. They emphasized subtle distinctions between apparently similar types, fiercely defending their choices against those of rival designers. The Swiss typographer Emil Ruder switched to Univers from Akzidenz Grotesk in 1957 when it was released and never looked back. Beginning in 1961 with the essay "Univers and Contemporary Typography" in *Typografische Monatsblätter*, he championed Adrian Frutiger's breakthrough design over a series of issues. Ruder viewed Univers as the ideal sans serif, neither derived from the past (as was Helvetica) nor entirely divorced from it (as was Futura).

Not only did Univers become Ruder's sole typeface, but he bequeathed his passion for it to several of his students, most notably Helmut Schmid. For over 40 years, Schmid, who is based in Osaka, Japan, has preached the gospel of Ruder, including the exclusive use of Univers. It can be seen in *The Road to Basel* as well as the special issue of *Idea* magazine devoted to Ruder that Schmid edited and designed. Similarly, Willi Kunz relies almost entirely on Univers. In *Typography: Macro- + Micro-Aesthetics*, he makes a case for it that has echoes of Ruder: "Univers has neither the rigid forms of Helvetica nor the geometric construction of Futura," he writes. And "unlike Gill and many other sans serif faces it comprises a series complete in terms of weights as well as widths. Univers, moreover, is quietly refined in its visual details." The issue of a large, consistent family of weights and widths was a key selling point prior to the advent of digital type.

The advocates for Univers were matched in passion and intensity, if not in unswerving devotion, by those loyal to Akzidenz Grotesk and Helvetica. Wolfgang Weingart, another Ruder student, perversely shunned Univers. "Too slick for my taste, I respected the design of Univers, but preferred the ruggedness of Akzidenz Grotesk," he writes in *My Way to Typography*, his typographic autobiography. Although the book is set in Times Roman, the work in it is almost exclusively set in Akzidenz Grotesk, most notably his covers for *Typografische Monatsblätter* between 1972 and 1976. Another designer who stuck with Akzidenz Grotesk after 1957 was Rudolph de Harak. He not only employed it for his iconic Westminster Records album covers and McGraw-Hill paperbacks; he also vigorously debated its merits with Massimo Vignelli.

Although Vignelli has frequently said that a designer needs only four (or five or six) typefaces, the single typeface that he is most identified with is Helvetica. He agitated for it from the moment he first discovered it as Neue Haas Grotesk in the late 1950s, eventually turning it into the house face at Unimark, from which it spread throughout the corporate world. Vignelli embraced Helvetica because it had no shoulders like other sans serifs, including Univers, and thus could be set very tightly without anyone having to cut up proofs. "And I started to use it and use it," he says, "and the more you use it, the more you learn how to use it. It's just like a piano: The more you play it, the more you learn how to play it, and the better player you become. And so it is with the type. And it is a great typeface. It will last forever."

The notion that using a typeface over and over enables a designer to become attuned to its virtues (and faults) is something other designers who believe in a limited type palette also stress. Jack Stauffacher, a book designer and the proprietor of the Greenwood Press, in San Francisco, has explored the nuances of the Janson types from size to size in metal for over a half century. His passion for Janson began in 1954 with *Janson: A Definitive Collection* and culminated decades later with the publication in 1983 of Gyorgy Haiman's *Nicholas Kis: A Hungarian Punch-Cutter and Printer, 1650–1702*, the book that definitively credited Kis as the author of the Janson types. Stauffacher's enthusiasm for Kis's types has been shared by several others, notably Wolfgang Tiessen, a German letterpress printer and book designer who began his career working with Gotthard de Beauclair at the Trajanus-Presse, the printing arm of D. Stempel AG, the foundry that revived the Janson types.

The Janson/Kis types are seen by their proponents as more sophisticated and unified than the better-known Caslon types. Yet Caslon, especially in metal, has its modern adherents as well. John Randle, owner of the Whittington Press and publisher of *Matrix*, has stuck with Caslon from the beginning of his career, taking to heart the old American printing maxim "When in doubt, set it in Caslon." What enthusiasts like about Caslon's faces is their quirkiness. As D.B. Updike memorably wrote, "Dutch founts were monotonous, but Caslon's founts were not so. His letters analysed are not perfect individually; but in mass their effect is agreeable. That is, I think, their secret—a perfection of the whole, derived from harmonious but not necessarily perfect individual letter-forms." The brilliance of Caslon in metal can be seen in Randle's *A Miscellany of Type* (1990).

While Updike celebrated Caslon for its comfortable and commonsense qualities, others have preferred types of elegance, most notably those of Giambattista Bodoni or Firmin Didot. Alexey Brodovitch, the art director of *Harper's Bazaar* from 1934 to 1958, made the Didones the epitome of fashion and elegance through his use of them. Although he is usually identified with Didot (a fact that led Fabien Baron to commission a new Didot from Jonathan Hoefler in the late 1980s as part of a revival of *Harper's Bazaar*), Brodovitch actually used a mix of Bodoni and Didot, sprinkled with other types in the neoclassical genre. He dedicated part of *Portfolio #1* (1950) to a paean to Bodoni.

The principal Bodoni protagonist has been the Italian publisher Franco Maria Ricci, who was born in Parma, the city where Bodoni became famous. Ricci started his career with the audacious publication in the mid-1960s of a three-volume facsimile of Bodoni's *Manuale Tipografico* (1818). He has said that he is fascinated by Bodoni, admiring his intelligence, his brightness, and "his ability to think in black-and-white, in perfect mathematical relations, his measure, the harmonic canons, the unity of the page."

A small cadre of designers believes that there is one perfect typeface, but in the larger world, the idea that a single one could approach perfection is doubtful. The perfect typeface might be a serif for some and a sans for others—though whether it is Akzidenz Grotesk, Helvetica, or Univers is open to debate. ∎

[Handwritten marginal notes visible in the layout]

Spread ❺: October 2011; Design: Ben King, *Print* art director.

CASE STUDY:

MONUMENTAL

Excerpts from *Monumental: The Reimagined World of Kevin O'Callaghan*

DEBORAH HUSSEY

Managing editor, School of Visual Arts, New York

When Alexander Calder's miniature circus was exhibited at the Whitney Museum in the early 1970s, the public was captivated. For fourteen-year-old Kevin O'Callaghan, the effects of seeing it were seismic. The circus characters were made from found objects and offered an amusing do-it-yourself quality, which Calder orchestrated through whimsical performances using his three-dimensional constructions. These creations were, in fact, intricately detailed and crafted with precision. Though small in size, Calder's "Circus" and its ringmaster served as principal influences for O'Callaghan's artistic evolution.

Working small or large scale, O'Callaghan always thinks big, weaving together visual narratives that offer new perspectives through the juxtaposition of the ordinary with the spectacular.

O'Callaghan's mother, Mary "Buddi" Steller, embraced the elaborate and the humorous, and had a flair for the theatrical —traits that were endowed upon her son. She met Kevin's father at the 1939 World's Fair, where Timothy O'Callaghan, a well-known architect, had designed several pavilions. In one of them, Steller, a showgirl for Billy Rose, was hired to strike and maintain a pose within a big golden frame. (Sixty-five years after the '39 World's Fair, O'Callaghan would create a gold-leaf frame to surround a mammoth television monitor that projects eclectic entertainment to its audience in the heart of Times Square.)

The attraction to the monumental coupled with an innate artistic talent are his father's legacy. In his architectural practice, which included contributions to the design of the Mets' Shea Stadium, the senior O'Callaghan strove to emphasize a fine-art aesthetic. Timothy O'Callaghan also created stage sets for producer Mike Todd, whose adaptation of *Around the World in 80 Days* is an apt metaphor for Kevin's tenacity and success in uncharted territory.

Completing his studies at the School of Visual Arts (SVA) in New York, O'Callaghan began searching for a career in advertising, his collegiate major and intended profession. Feeling disheartened by the perfunctory agency review process, in 1982 O'Callaghan created a colossal 3-D portfolio case that he drove around New York City, which gained him a two-page spread in *People* magazine and several job offers.

O'Callaghan's blossoming talent was cultivated at Dale Mallie's design studio, which specialized in making props for TV commercials. Up against an impossible deadline, Mallie,

↑ *Monumental* cover design by Mike Joyce.

the world, as far as I can see. There's a certain kind of playfulness about a lot of Kevin's students' work that just isn't there anywhere else, as well as his ability to get students to work extraordinary hours in compressed amounts of time to bring together an exhibition. Some of those things go on elsewhere, but nothing like what he does."

O'Callaghan conducts his classes in a large, open workspace filled with "let yourself go" energy and believes this is the best environment to foster creativity. While students work on projects individually, each is influenced by other students' craft. They see how well someone is doing something and then pick up the pace in their own projects. Typically, O'Callaghan sees the real learning experience in the final days before an opening: If students don't work together, rushing as a team to complete the final exhibition tasks, the show may be a failure, and they know it. His students leave his course understanding how to get a job done.

As an educator, O'Callaghan possesses a rare combination of indomitable fortitude and immeasurable tenderness. He is a demanding teacher who gives his students all that he can, and expects them to work at least as hard as he does in helping them to achieve their visions. The wisdom of everything in

whose work O'Callaghan had always admired, was looking for someone who could work all night to finish a job. Their conversation ended with a suggestion that O'Callaghan bring a toothbrush, since they would be working until dawn. In O'Callaghan's orbit, synchronicity is commonplace. He had just finished making a ten-foot toothbrush for a toothpaste ad and brought it along. He stayed well past sunrise, finishing the job, and then he worked at the studio for two months creating special effects for commercials and expanding his artistic skills. Achieving these effects in a pre-digital environment meant constructing them. O'Callaghan became known as the guy who could make huge objects and deliver them overnight. His ability to produce at warp speed is unparalleled. During a five-week period he created a carousel for MTV, worked on the ninetieth anniversary exhibition for Grand Central Terminal, and designed the AMC "TVs for Movie People" extravaganza.

In 1999, O'Callaghan founded the undergraduate 3-D design program at the School of Visual Arts, which he currently chairs. Addressing his educational initiatives, SVA president David Rhodes reflects, "There is nothing like it anywhere in

↑ Kevin O'Callaghan's first professional portfolio from *Monumental*.

↑ *Yugo Telephone*. **Artist:** Scott Lesiak.

moderation eludes O'Callaghan; his is a realm based upon the paradoxical, encompassing Foucault's "thinking the unthinkable" and Voltaire's reasoning that "the superfluous is a very necessary thing." He's been known to have a quick fuse under pressure and to react with verve, often accompanied by audible projection and a face as red as his hair.

Part cultural anthropologist and part creative whiz kid, O'Callaghan possesses a mature artistic vision that coexists with that cusp of life where the tooth fairy is alive and well, seductively inviting the fanciful to flourish. Yet for all the razzmatazz and grandeur that contribute to his creative ingenuity, he is a dignified and humble man, thoughtful and deliberate in his communication. When he shares an exploit, he becomes fully submerged in the moment, as though reliving the experience—the smells, colors, sights, and sounds.

Ultimately, O'Callaghan symphonies are composed of textured dialogues through which disparate elements are repurposed and interwoven: a moonman makes orange juice and discarded cell phones are transformed into an Earth Day tree. A master of the visual subtext, he summons audiences by constructing environments that invite individual interpretation of the artworks and their stories. Above all else is O'Callaghan's inextinguishable resolve to awaken the creative in each of us.

While many of his projects and commissions bring forth the whimsical, O'Callaghan also engages in social and political commentary. Each undertaking is supported by

the idea of taking obsolete objects and giving them new uses through creative reinvention. The 2009 "Off-Roading" project took a fuel-indulgent truck off the highway and gave it new life by converting its parts into household furnishings, including working lamps, chairs, tables, a couch, and a chaise longue. Off-Roading did not offer a solution to the problems of consumption and waste that plague contemporary culture, but it was a vehicle, literal and otherwise, for contemplation of these pressing matters.

Sounding a call to arms that embrace, O'Callaghan mounted the acclaimed "Disarm" exhibition in 2006, which repurposed M16 assault rifles into icons of a nonviolent society: the sanctity of a white picket fence, the sounds of a violin, and the security of a teddy bear. O'Callaghan's humanitarian beliefs are expressed in *Art is ... Healing*, a poster he created in response to the World Trade Center devastation of September 11, 2001. The poster is part of the permanent collection of the Library of Congress in Washington, D.C.

The narrative accompaniment to the images on these pages offers a background to the brilliant mosaic that is O'Callaghan. The anecdotes have been gleaned from the artist as well as from the shared experiences of his collaborators and colleagues. Their reflections speak to a career that has spanned three decades and continues to surprise and delight.

↑ *Yugo Confessional*. **Artist:** Ann Marie Mattioli. **Photography:** Tia Magallon.

Introductions also reveal the intent and style of the writer

ⓠⓐ Deborah Hussey Talks about Writing for Books

You wrote the introduction to the book *Monumental: The Reimagined World of Kevin O'Callaghan*. What is the purpose of an introduction to this or any book?

Introductions differ with each project. In broad strokes, they serve as detailed content lists and a road map that highlights what will be explored, as well as any notable landmarks the reader will encounter along the way—like an amuse-bouche that sets the stage for the entrée. Introductions also reveal the intent and style of the writer. It is here where the author's opinions and topics of personal importance or interest are acknowledged.

What do you write in an introduction that will not appear elsewhere in the book?

I find it works best to write the introduction after the rest of the book has been drafted. At this point, you have collected all of your research and know what's been covered, so you can make informed decisions about the intro: What should (or should not) be outlined, emphasized, stated, or reiterated.

Because *Monumental* was intended to give a balanced narrative that encompassed the creative process, student and professional work, exhibition designs, and teaching methods, it was important that the introduction offer an historical background on Kevin O'Callaghan, whose work is featured in *Monumental*, as this would not be emphasized in the essays. It was also essential to Kevin for this history to include a nod to some of the instrumental people in his life. Also, the introduction was the only opportunity for outlining the range and scope of Kevin's initiatives and accomplishments, and the occasion to convey a fully developed and cohesive portrait of the artist (as both a young and not-so-young man).

How do you capture the key qualities of your subject in the short amount of space allotted?

The key qualities were based on the book's initiatives: a tribute to Kevin's talents as an artist and an educator, and the remarkable achievements of his students. Added to this foundation were the guiding principles by which Kevin has attained his numerous successes. These essential ingre-

dients revealed themselves through interviews with his colleagues and collaborators. Fortunately, these were all related elements that could be smoothly woven together as a coherent whole within the space restrictions.

In this introduction, what are the most important parts and how did you construct them?

Communicating Kevin's innate ability and brilliance in seeing everyday objects and seamlessly transforming them into otherworldly forms was paramount. His passion and inimitable creative process were of obvious significance, as was the importance that repurposing objects has for Kevin. His stoic work ethic and commitment to collaboration and community were also important. Kevin is known for his affection for pop culture references and for his love of the sensational, so I thought it important to highlight some of the more politically and socially motivated exhibition themes, such as the *Disarm* show about the tragic destruction of assault weapons. Collective anecdotes seemed the best approach in constructing and capturing the quintessential O'Callaghan.

Endings are always as difficult as beginnings. How did you achieve success with both?

From the very first conversation I had with Kevin about his practice, it was clear that the book needed to start with his initial reaction to the works of Alexander Calder—specifically Calder's *Circus*, which was Kevin's creative awakening. For all of the wonderful O'Callaghan stories that I was told during the project, several of which were also suitable as beginnings, it always circled back to *Circus*.

The book's ending was equally apparent from early in the process. The magnificent and monumental "Turn of the Century" carousel contained all of the elements that both characterize and distinguish Kevin's talent and practice. From its humble raw materials of blue foam and rusted parts, its metamorphosis stands as a crowning achievement to an illustrious career.

CASE STUDY:

END OF THE GLUE-POT ERA

An Editing Process in Three Versions

STEVEN HELLER

The essay that follows, commissioned by the editors at *Print* magazine, went through three edits. The first iteration included many quotations solicited from well-known designers. These quotations were originally integrated into the body of the text. However, after a close reading by the copy editor, he felt the flow of the narrative was disconcertingly interrupted by the quotes. So, in the second version, they were removed. Still, the quotes were a necessary component of the story, and I did not want to lose them. In the final version, they were edited to remove redundancy and reintroduced on their own, published on a separate page with my text used to introduce them. Since this is an essay on how technology has altered design practice, I also wanted to call it "Not Your Mother's Graphic Design." The editor, as is his prerogative, changed that too. You be the judge of what worked the best.

ORIGINAL VERSION

When graphic design was not brain surgery, it was much easier to practice. The new graphic (or shall we say cross-platform, multidisciplinary) design is more neurologically complex than at any other time in history. Arguably, it is more like brain surgery now—minus the life and death consequences. Nonetheless, today's graphic design is not your mother's graphic design (unless your mother is 20-something). It is no longer possible to launch a graphic design career with a ruler, X-Acto, and glue pot on a kitchen table (although a laptop would fit nicely).

Ken Carbone (co-founder, chief creative director, Carbone Smolan) notes, "Twenty or thirty years ago, graphic design was the domain of a select group of practitioners highly trained in disciplines ranging from corporate identity and editorial design to packaging and environmental graphics. They were based in design hubs in major cities such as New York, Chicago, Los Angeles and San Francisco here in the USA and select cities abroad. All was good. The advent of the computer ushered in the "Great Design Democracy," and the ranks of graphic designers exploded. Now, great designers can be found in every 300-square-foot office around the globe, offering an expanded range of digital and interactive design services requiring new tools and new thinking. The barriers of entry to the profession no longer exist. Design is now a commodity business forcing "seasoned" design firms to quickly adapt to the heightened competition. Clients benefit from this and have more choice. Having a 'contemporary' suite of design services keeps you in the game. However, the key to winning has not changed. Fresh talent, great design, solid client service, and the color red still breed success."

Engineering has made progressive design concepts from decades ago more economically doable. Massimo Vignelli recently said about his flawed, yet revolutionary, 1972 New York City subway map, that it was an "A.C. (after computer) design in a B.C. (before computer) world." The map was recently relaunched as an online interactive diagram by NYC's Metropolitan Transportation Authority, with all the bugs worked out—forty years later. New technologies have given and taken away. They have impacted designer and client perceptions and anticipations. They have altered the fundamental approach to business and even how new revenue streams are acquired. They have transformed designers from service providers to entrepreneurs. There are so many variants in this new flux that I asked some veteran graphic designers—those who have lived in the B.C. and A.C. worlds—to reflect on how "change" has altered their respective practices (and sometimes, their lives).

Jonathan Hoefler (president, Hoefler Frere-Jones) also identifies the past quarter century as a massive redirect of the industry: "Both the practice of typeface design and the obligations of the designer have become considerably more complex in the past few decades. Twenty years ago, digital type was

in its infancy and type design was a charming cottage industry: independent designers, often working in isolation, could invent ideas for typefaces, produce them on the desktop, and supply them to nearby art directors. Today, the burdens of the entire world weigh down on the profession. Both our clients and their readers are distributed throughout the world, making the linguistic demands placed upon a typeface ever greater, and the requirement that typefaces function on a diverse and explosively growing number of platforms makes them ever more complicated to engineer and manufacture. A profession of one-man-bands has developed into an industry of organized specialists, not unlike the way the profession evolved between the era of independent type founder Claude Garamond and the advent of the Mergenthaler Linotype Company. But that evolution took 350 years, and what we've experienced has taken scarcely two decades."

Digital tools and what they hath wrought are the first obvious differences. Only Gutenberg's invention of the printing press is on a par. In fact, what would Herr Gutenberg say if he saw perfect type on an iPad screen? Granted, tools are always changing but, as we are frequently reminded by historians and futurists alike, digital tools and platforms have markedly and eternally impacted the seminal definition of design like never before. So what is different, exactly?

Reflecting on the discreet ways these tools have affected his practice, Nicholas Blechman (art director, the *New York Times Book Review*) suggests, "The profession has shifted in subtle ways, mostly in how designers promote themselves and interact with each other. Bulky black portfolios have been replaced with slick iPads, and postcard promos with PDF attachments. I no longer keep artists' handouts on file, but instead bookmark [Adobe] Illustrator sites in Safari. I spend more time art directing through email than on the phone."

Designers still conceptualize using their own brains. That has stayed fairly constant since before the advent of printing. Designers' tastes have also remained fairly subjective, though routinely tied to the fashions and styles of the dominant (or alpha) designer.

Well, one thing that's new is "design thinking." Hmmmm. Just a couple of decades ago, before the term was coined, design thinking might have been called "conceptualizing" or "strategizing" or even "designing." Today, it is a distinct discipline along with "design innovation," another catch-term that raises designer status above lower primates. Seriously though, these terms did not just materialize because a motivational speaker needed a hook to hang his aspirations on.

Jessica Helfand (co-founder, Winterhouse) looks to her teaching for answers: "I tend to notice the changes in the profession less in terms of my own work and more in terms of the shifts in my students. There was a time in the early 1990s when the then-new media skewed not only the perspectives of young designers, but also the economic environment within which they flourished. (As new opportunities proliferated so, too, did the fat wallets that supported them.) Budgets ballooned, and so did egos—and none of it made for work that was that transformative or memorable or great. Leaner times make for better designers. More meaningful work, and greater challenges."

Digital technologies have made it possible to increase the scope of design practice a hundred fold. It is not enough to just instinctually make stuff. Design (including traditional graphic design) is more integrated than ever into the daily lives of us all.

Cheryl Towler Weese (founder, creative director, Studio Blue) states, "One shift I've noticed is that in many projects, we've moved from creating narrative to developing an informational toolbox or dashboard. Working in interactive media has given us greater control over how information is organized (formerly, a role that fell within a writer's or editor's purview). I think the development of new media has shaken up roles and allowed cross-fertilization. Clients are also recognizing the value of social entrepreneurship and the role that strategy and change management can play in the front end of design." Might that be more communicative power in the hands of mere individuals than even he could handle? Mr. McLuhan, can you answer that?

Together with engineers, and others, designers are now developing, not just making, things. The capacity to make design move in various dimensions is no longer a novelty—it's a necessity. According to Stefan Sagmeister (owner, Sagmeister

Inc.), "The still image will continue to lose in importance, everything that can be animated will be animated—not always to the advantage of the quality of the project."

If there is one (drum-roll) fundamental change, among all others, it is that graphic design is now time- and space-based. Understanding the storytelling arc is essential in making analog and digital design. How to move the viewer's over-taxed eye from point A to B to Z—over time, through space, and via motion and interaction—is a skill that was once relatively minor. Increased data flow has made narration the primary directive. Graphic designers always thought about the end product on their audience, but now "User Experience" is the mantra.

At Martha Stewart Omni Media, chief creative officer Gael Towey traced the early evolution of *Martha Stewart Living* meets user experience: "In November of 2010, we introduced our first iPad issue of *Martha Stewart Living* called 'Boundless Beauty.' It wasn't available in print and it contained all new stories. This was our 'beta' test for creating simultaneous digital versions of our regular monthly issues, which we launched the following January for *Martha Stewart Living* and *Everyday Food*. For our 'Boundless Beauty' issue we created stories that took advantage of the new functionality available with the iPad. The issue had five videos and many slide shows, scrolls, panoramas, and animations. We created stories that would showcase these new functionalities; for example, the before-and-after beauty story, the puff pastry story where you touch the screen and it opens before your eyes, a peony story where you can glide you finger across the panorama of Martha's garden. Working with these extra features is liberating, as a how-to brand. The opportunities to be able to show before and after, step-by-step slide shows makes it even easier to entice the reader and easier to teach them. It was also relatively easy for our staff to make the transition to video since we are also a TV company; most of the senior staff has been on Martha's show, so we understood what was required to make good video. However, we also had to produce video on a shoestring; in other words, not like TV. Our still photographers were eager to work with us because their businesses are changing and many of them are enjoying the new cameras that allow you to shoot still and video with the same camera. There are also lots of new tools to help make shooting video work, like shoulder harnesses for handheld and extra audio equipment. This is the changing world of publishing: our technology tools are giving us more flexibility than ever, and we can tell stories in ways that give more dimension, texture, emotional impact, and information. Our monthly digital issues contain moving covers (think Harry Potter); how-to videos where you may learn about a particular vegetable in the farmer's market, or learn how to make a weeknight meal of four recipes in three minutes, or you may just have fun looking at our stop-action well openers that are always surprising and delightful. All of this does require new training and, mostly, a curiosity and willingness to solve problems differently."

I reckon if El Lissitzky, Piet Zwart or even Paul Rand (who owned a computer) returned from Valhalla to resume their practice, they wouldn't recognize the design field.

FIRST EDITED VERSION

When graphic design was not brain surgery, it was much easier to practice. The new graphic—or shall we say, cross-platform, multi-disciplinary—design is more neurologically complex than at any other time in history. Arguably, it is more like brain surgery now—minus the life and death consequences. Nonetheless, today's graphic design is not your mother's graphic design (unless your mother is 20-something). I reckon if El Lissitzky, Piet Zwart or even Paul Rand (who owned a computer) returned from Valhalla to resume their practice, they wouldn't recognize the design field.

The first obvious differences are digital tools and what they hath wrought. Only Gutenberg's invention of the printing press is on a par. But what is different, exactly? Designers still conceptualize using their own brains. That has remained fairly constant since before printing. Designers' tastes remain fairly subjective, though routinely tied to the fashions and styles of the dominant or alpha-designer. These happen to be the key ingredients in "design thinking," right?

One thing that's new is . . . "design thinking." Just a couple of decades ago, design thinking might have been called "conceptualizing" or "strategizing" or even "designing." Today it is a distinct discipline along with "design innovation," another catch-term that raises designers' status above lower primates. These terms did not just materialize because a motivational speaker needed a hook to hang his motivations on.

Digital technologies have made it possible to increase the scope of design practice a hundred fold. Design is more inte-grated into daily life. Engineering has made visionary design concepts from decades ago more economically doable today. Massimo Vignelli recently said about his flawed yet revolutionary 1972 NYC subway map, that it was [an] "A.C. (after computer) design in a B.C. (before computer world)." The map was recently re-launched as an online interactive diagram by NYC's Metropolitan Transportation Authority, with all the bugs worked out—forty years later.

The capacity to make design move in various dimensions is no longer a novelty, it's a necessity. If there is one (drumroll) fundamental change, among all others, it is that graphic design is now time-and-space-based. Understanding the storytelling arc is essential in making analog and digital design. How to move the viewer's over-taxed eye from point A to B to Z over time and space and via motion and interaction is a skill that was once relatively minor. Increased data flow has made narration the primary directive. Graphic designers always thought about the end product, but now User Experience is the mantra.

The new technologies have given and taken away. They have altered the fundamental approach to business, how new revenue streams are acquired, and transformed designers from service providers to entrepreneurs. There are so many variants in this flux that I asked some veteran graphic designers—those who have lived in the B.C. and A.C. worlds—to reflect on how "change" has altered their respective practices (and sometimes, their lives).

FINAL EDITED VERSION

When graphic design was not brain surgery, it was much easier to practice. The new graphic—or, shall we say, cross-platform, multidisciplinary—design is more neurologically complex than at any other time in history. Arguably, it is more like actual brain surgery now (minus the life-and-death consequences), with as complicated a network of synapses to navigate as anything you'll find in your head. It is no longer possible to launch a graphic design career with a ruler, an X-[A]cto blade, and a glue pot on your kitchen table. I'd bet that if El Lissitzky, Piet Zwart, or even Paul Rand (who owned a computer) returned from Valhalla to resume their practices, they wouldn't recognize the design field.

The obvious engine for these changes is digital tools and what they have wrought. Only Gutenberg's invention of the printing press is on a par. Digital technologies have made it possible [to] increase the scope of design practice a hundred fold. Design is now tightly integrated into our daily lives, and engineering has made visionary design concepts from decades past more feasible. Massimo Vignelli told me that his flawed yet revolutionary 1972 NYC subway map was "created in B.C. (before computer) for the A.C. (after computer) era." The map was recently relaunched as an online interactive diagram by NYC's Metropolitan Transportation Authority, with all the bugs worked out—40 years later.

The capacity to make design move in multiple dimensions is no longer a novelty; it's a necessity. Because if there is one fundamental effect of technology, among all the others, it is that graphic design is now time-and-space-based. Understanding the storytelling arc is essential in making analog and digital design alike. Knowing how to move the viewer's overtaxed eye from point A to B to Z is a skill that was once relatively minor. Increased data flow has turned narration into the primary function of design. Graphic designers have always thought about their audience, but now "user experience" is their mantra.

The new technologies have also altered how designers approach doing business, often transforming them from service providers to entrepreneurs. But since there are so many varia-

↑ *Final Article* in *Print* magazine, December 2011.

tions in this flux that I asked some veteran graphic designers—those who have lived in both the B.C. and A.C. worlds—to reflect on how the last decade has altered their practices and, sometimes, their lives.

(continued from page 36)

Jessica Helfand,
Winterhouse, New Haven,
Connecticut
"I tend to notice the changes in the profession less in terms of my own work and more in terms of the shifts in my students'. There was a time in the early 1990s when the then-new media skewed not only the perspectives of young designers but the economic environment within which they flourished. (As new opportunities proliferated, so, too, did the fat wallets that supported them.) Budgets ballooned, and so did egos—and none of it made for work that was that transformative or memorable or great. Leaner times make for better designers, more meaningful work, and greater challenges."

Cheryl Towler Weese,
Studio Blue, Chicago
"One shift I've noticed is that in many projects, we've moved from creating narrative to developing an informational toolbox or dashboard. Working in interactive media has given us greater control over how information is organized—formerly, a role that fell within a writer or editor's purview. I think the development of new media has shaken up roles and allowed cross-fertilization. Clients are also recognizing the value of social entrepreneurship and the role that strategy and change management can play in the front end of design."

Nicholas Blechman,
The New York Times Book
Review, *New York City*
"The profession has shifted in subtle ways, mostly in how designers promote themselves and interact with each other. Bulky black portfolios have been replaced with slick iPads, and postcard promos with PDF attachments. I no

longer keep artists' handouts on file but instead bookmark illustrator sites in Safari. I spend more time art directing through email than on the phone."

Jonathan Hoefler,
Hoefler Frere-Jones,
New York City
"Both the practice of typeface design and the obligations of the designers have become considerably more complex in the past few decades. Twenty years ago, digital type was in its infancy and type design was a charming cottage industry. Independent designers, often working in isolation, could invent ideas for typefaces, produce them on the desktop, and supply them to nearby art directors. Today, the burdens of the entire world weigh down on the profession. Both our clients and their readers are distributed throughout the world, making the linguistic demands placed upon a typeface ever greater; and the requirement that typefaces function on a diverse and explosively growing number of platforms makes them evermore complicated to engineer and manufacture. A profession of

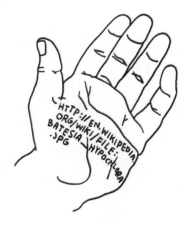

one-man bands has developed into an industry of organized specialists, not unlike the way the profession evolved between the era of independent typefounder Claude Garamond, and the advent of the Mergenthaler Linotype Company. But that evolution took 350 years, and what we've experienced has taken scarcely two decades."

Gael Towey, *Martha Stewart*
Omnimedia, New York City
"In November 2010, we introduced our first iPad issue of *Martha Stewart Living,* called 'Boundless Beauty.' It wasn't available in print, and it contained all-new stories. This was our beta test for creating simultaneous digital versions of our regular monthly issues, which we launched the following January for *Martha Stewart Living* and *Everyday Food.* For 'Boundless Beauty,' we took advantage of the new functionality available with the iPad with videos, slide shows, scrolls, panoramas, and animations. We created stories that would showcase these new functionalities (e.g., a peony story where you can glide you finger across a panorama of Martha's garden).

Being able to show before-and-after, step-by-step slide shows makes it even easier to entice readers and teach them. All of this does require new training and mostly a curiosity and willingness to solve problems differently."

Ken Carbone,
Carbone Smolan Agency,
New York City
"Twenty or thirty years ago, graphic design was the domain of a select group of highly trained practitioners in disciplines ranging from corporate identity and editorial design to packaging and environmental graphics. They were based in design hubs such as New York, Chicago, Los Angeles, and San Francisco and select cities abroad. All was good.

The advent of the computer ushered in the Great Design Democracy, and the ranks of graphic designers exploded. Now, great designers can be found in every 300-square-foot office around the globe, offering an expanded range of digital and interactive design services requiring new tools and new thinking. The barriers of entry to the profession no longer exist. Design is now a commodity business forcing 'seasoned' design firms to quickly adapt to the heightened competition. Clients benefit from this and have more choice. Having a 'contemporary' suite of design services keeps you in the game. However, the key to winning has not changed. Fresh talent, great design, solid client service, and the color red still breed success."

Stefan Sagmeister,
Sagmeister Inc.,
New York City
"The still image will continue to lose in importance, and everything that can be animated will be animated—not always to the advantage of the quality of the project." ∎

LEARNING
FROM
EXPERIENCES

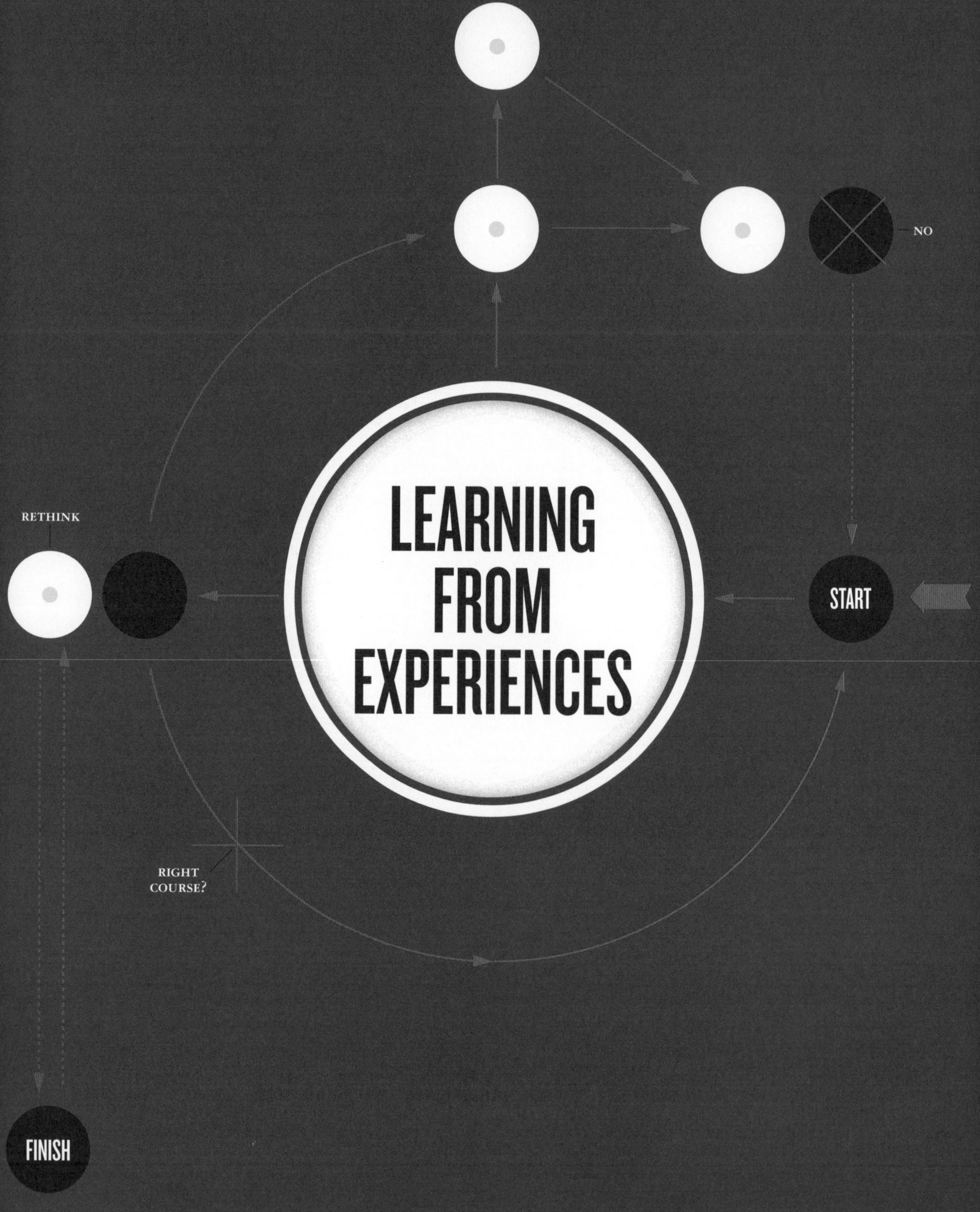

RETHINK

START

NO

RIGHT
COURSE?

FINISH

Learning comes from doing. One must write every day, even twice a day, to get the feel of words, the tenor of voice and a sense of flow. Writing theory is fine, but without the hands-on experience, without reading what is written — outloud to oneself — writing as an extension of the writer is impossible to achieve. Most writers have written a lot before ever getting published. A published work is usually polished — made to shine — before being released to the public. But unpolished writing is a means to that ends. Experience builds over time.

Some of the most respected writers on design today agreed to share a favorite or telling essay, article, blog post, or paper and then discuss their process. The following case studies and interviews provide a vivid opportunity to learn from their experiences.

The first is about the success of failure. It is designed to inspire and caution. Other essays in this section cover a wide range of design and popular-culture themes. Read them carefully, and make notes in the margins (i.e., if there is a thought that is confusing or a question unanswered). Use these essays as a kind of workbook for your own writing. Then read the sidebar interviews to ascertain whether some of your questions have been answered.

CASE STUDY:
ON FAILURE

 ALLAN CHOCHINOV

Editor-in-chief of *Core77* and chair of MFA Products of Design, School of Visual Arts, New York
(Originally pulished in Design Disasters *{Allworth Press, 2008})*

For all the talk of the value of learning through failure, it is difficult to get the concept across if we continue to use the word "failure" in that sentence. People have a natural aversion to the term, and it is next to impossible to reclaim it for pedagogic purposes.

For all the talk of the value of learning through failure, what we really mean is that it is valuable to do something multiple times, learning lessons from each attempt and applying those lessons to subsequent versions. This is a tough bargain, requiring both patience and diligence, and not a little thick skin.

For all the talk of the value of learning through failure, it is in the rewards of persistence where the true lessons lie. And the lessons of persistence can only be learned by those who persist—a kind of chicken and egg conundrum that can never be solved, save by those who, you guessed it, can tolerate failure.

For all the talk of the value of learning through failure, it is really the notion of iteration that we should be concentrating on. It is the repeated doing of a thing that makes it better—not unlike learning any skill—but this is a difficult thing to get across to designers. They are pleased to get a thing done even once, never mind multiple times.

For all the talk of the value of learning through failure, it is iteration that should be up on the marquee. But it is not so much the "teaching" of iteration that we're talking about; rather, it is the appreciation of iteration. And this requires a stern but empathetic taskmaster, first external, but in the end, from deep inside.

For all the talk of the value of learning through failure, the quest for perfection is what we're really talking about here. It is the doing and redoing of a thing that gets one close to the ideal—removing the extraneous and preserving the essential—ultimately driving something toward its elemental, rarefied state.

For all the talk of the value of learning

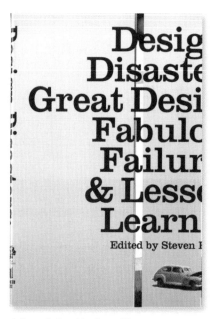

↑ Cover designed by James Victore.

through failure, it is the pursuit of success that fuels the fire. In trying to succeed at something, we are destined to miss the mark on occasion, but to say that every time we fall short of "success" we "fail" is l ike saying that every time we don't win a baseball game we lose one. Wait, I guess that is saying that.

Writing about contemporary design culture often means having to go head to head with individuals who you consider to be implicated in harmful or inane design activity. . . .

For all the talk of the value of learning through failure, it is really humility at the heart of the matter. It takes guts to recognize when something isn't working, and bravery to attempt to do it again. It is the calling on these emotional components that make "failure the best teacher," not the successful or less-than-successful completion of the task at hand.

For all the talk of the value of learning through failure, it is the concept of rigor that deserves the discourse. And although it is often the first gesture which, in the end, remains standing as the best, rigorous investigation through multiple variations, if not generating better alternatives, will, at the very least, confirm what was first best all along.

For all the talk of the value of learning through failure, it is difficult to get the concept across if we continue to use the word "failure" in that sentence. People have a natural aversion to the term, and it is next to impossible to reclaim it for pedagogic purposes.

ℚ/ⓐ Allan Chochinov Talks about the Writer's Attitude

What was your motivation to write this article?

I was thinking about the theme of the book and how, for designers, the notion of learning through failure was a true yet frightfully clichéd idea. Instead of some thoughts or discourse, I figured I might try to actually demonstrate it in the text itself. It didn't take long to come upon the idea that the last paragraph would be identical to the first, since that it's also true too often — that our first idea is our best. Anecdotally, I don't think all readers register these bookends, though, so perhaps a bit of a failure… in the end.

What is the value of repetition in a written piece?

I've always felt that repetition will let you get away with murder. I play music, and so if I'm doing a solo on guitar and I mess up, I just repeat the mess-up two more times (three's the key) and then it seems totally intentional. It's the same in oration or ad pitches, or really anything. Humans crave patterns, and they're pattern seekers, and they really get a lot out of seeing things over and over, and repetition is a really, really great way of driving home a point.

How does your writing process differ from your design process?

That's a great question. The palette is different, at least for me; I've always been more verbal than visual. But I like making things, and when I'm making something I'm almost not thinking at all. I'm not sure that that kind of blank flow happens in my writing, though. I give myself lots of games to play and external constraints when I write. (I have a series of "1000 Word" essays that each have exactly 1,000 words in them.) I don't really need to do that in design because design is such an obvious puzzle to begin with. So I guess I've made them the same by puzzle-izing them both. So to answer your question: They may differ, but not if I have anything to do with it.

Does the act of writing often change the way you look at the topic/issue at hand?

Oh, of course. It may be true that there are two kinds of writers: those who need to know where they're going and those whose entire fun is in the getting there. The first creates outlines and plotlines and diagrams; knows the end at the beginning. The other kind, in comparison, seems downright reckless, but frankly, I couldn't imagine it any other way.

CASE STUDY:

TO WRITE ABOUT DESIGN IS TO CARE ABOUT OTHER PEOPLE

 DAVID BARRINGER

Freelance writer, editor, and publisher

You do not have to care about other people. You can choose to care about only yourself. You can make things for yourself and no one else. You can work for yourself and refuse to work for a client.

Instead, you can keep things to yourself. You can make things and hang them up around your room and call it a day. Call it a life. You don't have to care about anything, if you don't care to.

I care. I care about other people. I care about making things. I care about dreaming and thinking and writing and making. I care about graphic design and design culture. I care about what other designers are thinking, what they're making, how they're making it, how they're giving their designs to other people, and why they're working the way they're working. I care about how other people receive those designs, those messages, and those products. I care about how we talk to each other and how we relate to each other. I care about how we define value and create value and esteem the value in our work and in ourselves.

That's why I write. That's why I write about design. That's why I write about designers and other people and the culture.

You don't have to care. You don't have to write. You don't have to design. You don't have to evaluate the work of others. You don't have to evaluate your own work. You don't have to esteem the value of design or the value of work or the value of other people.

In fact, you don't have to make any judgments at all. You can regard everything and everyone as having the same value. You don't have to judge between two websites, two logos, two products, or two posters. You don't have to care who made them, how they were made, why they were made, what they look like, how they work, or who they're for. If you don't care, then you can't tell the difference. To you, they're all the same. One logo is as good as another. One magazine is as good as another. One designer is as good as another. One company is as good as another. One government is as good as another. Who cares?

If you don't care, you don't have to differentiate between a poster promoting this presidential candidate and a poster promoting that presidential candidate. They're both posters, they're both candidates, and you're not voting anyway (you don't care). If you don't care, you don't have to differentiate between store packaging for aspirin and street packaging for heroin. You don't have to differentiate between a website promoting sex with adults and a website promoting sex with minors. You don't have to differentiate between shareware and spyware, email and spam, or homage and plagiarism. You pretty much don't have to pay attention to anything: not form or aesthetics, not content or copyright, not paper or people. Does a design hurt someone or help someone? Is it ugly or beautiful? Is it well made or poorly made? Well, who cares? You don't have the desire to tell the difference. You don't criticize. You don't evaluate. You don't care.

Wow, this paper has great texture. That logo is well proportioned. Aren't these colors amazing? This website frustrates the user. That photo demeans the model. These signs are easy to read, even at a distance. That poster provokes a double-take. This overwrought packaging insults the intelligence. The ornaments on this book cover are beautifully mysterious.

Hey, wait a minute. What are you doing? Are you noticing things? The minute you start to notice things is the minute you start to care. It's the minute you start to care about design. It's the minute you start to care about other people. It's the minute you start to think, to evaluate, and to criticize.

I notice things, and I care. You notice things, and, if you're honest with yourself, you care too. So write about that. I want to notice what you notice. I want to care about what you care about. I can't be everywhere at once. I can't live any life but my own. By reading about the experiences of others, however, I can see more, feel more, and think more than I ever could on my own. By reading, I feel like I can live more than one life. You notice and write, and I read and imagine, and we both feel our lives grow larger and deeper.

ⓠ⁄ⓐ David Barringer Talks about Respect for the Reader

How important is the first paragraph, and what do you try to get into it?

The essay doesn't have a strict form. Like the novel, the essay changes with the times, the culture, the writer, the purpose. So there's no set thing as "the first paragraph." The opener could begin in the title, as in "This Essay Is about My First…" and then the first line finishes the thought with "…textual encounter." Or the champagne bottle of a single word could smash the prow and launch the essay. Or a musical note, a quote, an image, a doodle, a line of dialogue, a Q that begets an A, and so forth. The opening sets the tone, form, voice, perspective, and more. I can write a funny first-person essay about living with the affliction called "designer's eye." I can write a sober third-person essay about three graphic designers whose aesthetic nagging alienated their friends. The opening of the essay establishes which of these two essays I chose to write. And chose is probably too neutral a term for the dynamic that drives me to write. I have to be fired up and excited to write. I may try some new kind of form, some new opening (new to me), that casts a light into the tunnel.

If the first paragraph is important, what about the last;?

I don't have a method for ending essays. Most of my method takes place in the middle, not the beginning or the end. Beginnings often frame the question, and endings answer it in some way, literally or figuratively. The middle poses the greatest challenge, because in the middle the writer has to think. The writer thinks through writing. The writer states a claim and backs it up. Then the writer states a counterclaim and explores that. The writer questions every step in the argument. The writer has to worry about being misunderstood, about relying on solid and relevant evidence, about evaluating fairly and fully, and about avoiding poor arguments, like name calling, wishful thinking, lazy fact checking, and snarky whining. Writing is thinking, and thinking is hard, and you think through writing in the thick of the essay: smack in the middle.

What do you try to accomplish in a rewrite?

I rewrite with humility about my powers and respect for the reader's intelligence. I am afraid of being misunderstood. I often write, "I don't mean that. I mean this." I also have this anxiety that I overlooked a mistake somewhere: an error of judgment, an irrelevant comparison, an assumption that somebody did something when really someone else did it. If you are not humble, then you are likely to believe that whatever you have written is good. If you do not respect the reader, then you are likely to believe that whatever you have written is good enough. I reread before I rewrite. I reread my essays to see if I understand what I wrote. Respecting the reader means that I reread my work and ask, "Would a first-time reader understand this?" I rewrite until I'm less afraid of being misunderstood, less anxious about missing a mistake, and a little more confident that the reader will appreciate what I've tried to say and how I've tried to say it. Not only do I rewrite dozens of times; I will often abandon an essay or throw it all away and start again. I let time be my editor. I let essays sit there for months. I let books—entire books—sit on my hard drive indefinitely. If I don't believe my writing is good, then I don't believe anyone needs to read it.

CASE STUDY:

THE LANGUAGE OF DESIGN IMPERIALISM

MARIA POPOVA

Blogger and writer on design for *Wired UK* and *The Atlantic*
(*Originally published July 29, 2010 on Change Observer,*
http://changeobserver.designobserver.com/feature/the-language-of-design-imperialism/14718/)

I go to a lot of conferences. Design conferences, tech conferences, media conferences, cross-disciplinary conferences. And the worst of them are always the ones brimming with panels, on which a handful of industry heavy-hitters sit around for an hour, throwing opinions at each other that oscillate between congratulatory and contrarian but inevitably dance around a hermetic subject of collectively predetermined importance. The problem with such panels is that they regurgitate existing viewpoints held within the industry bubble about issues framed by the industry paradigm, often in buzzword-encrusted language that offers little substance beyond the collective fluff-slinging.

Over the past few weeks, the design community has witnessed the virtual version of an industry panel. Ignited by Bruce Nussbaum's controversial, and some may say solely for the sake thereof, contention that humanitarian designers are the new imperialists and followed by a flurry of responses ranging from insightful, fact-grounded retorts to righteous indignation to argumentative defensiveness, the debate has brought up some necessary conversations, but it has also become a platform for near-academic discussion of an issue tragically removed from the actual cultural landscapes where humanitarian design projects live. What's most worrisome and ironic about the debate is the almost complete lack — with the exception of a few blog comments here and there — of voices of designers who work in the very regions and communities in question, those loosely defined as the "developing world" and the "Western poor." Worse yet, entirely missing are the much-needed multidisciplinary voices whose work is the cultural glue between design and its social implementation — anthropologists, scientists, educators, writers.

Yes, writers.

Because if designers are the new imperialists, the delusional white-caped superheroes Nussbaum calls them out to be, design writers are their giddy, overeager sidekicks, complicit

We slide across a spectrum of political quasi-correctness and tragic generalization, from the near-obsolete for reasons of clear condescension "third world" to the hardly better "developing world"....

in disengaging from the very communities in which humanitarian design is meant to be manifest.

The way we talk and write about these issues is incredibly important. As [Nussbaum's] excellent *Wall Street Journal* article argues, language shapes culture and cognition in a powerful way. The very vocabulary we use in this debate is incredibly flawed. We can't even come up with a fair way of describing the communities in question. We slide across a spectrum of political quasi-correctness and tragic generalization, from the near-obsolete for reasons of clear condescension "third world" to the hardly better "developing world" to Alex Steffen's alarmingly geo-generalized "Global South" to the depressingly hierarchical "bottom billion." These lump terms not only dehumanize entire classes of people, but they also fail to account for the vast cultural differences between the various microcommunities within these brackets. Political, anthropological, ethnic, religious, and sociological differences that would explain why, for instance, the XO-1 laptop from One Laptop Per Child, once hailed as a pinnacle of humanitarian design, was embraced in Paraguay and reviled in India.

We talk about working "in the field" as the ultimate litmus test for true "humanitarian design." But the notion of "the field" flattens out an incredibly rich, layered, multiplane social system in which these design projects and products live. No wonder we consistently fail to design what Emily Pilloton aptly terms "systems, not stuff."

I'd be curious to know how these communities and cultures verbalize their own sense of self and identity. How do you say "bottom billion" in Swahili? How does "the field" describe itself in Aymara?

Even the term humanitarian design bespeaks a fundamental limitation—incredibly anthropocentric, it fails to recognize the importance of design that lives in a complex ecosystem of humanity and nature, society and environment, which are always symbiotically linked to one another's well-being. When even our language exudes the kind of cultural conceit that got us in our climate crisis pickle, there's something fundamentally wrong with how we think about our role in the world—as designers and as people.

In a brilliant *SEED* Magazine article from 2008, authors Maywa Montenegro and Terry Glavin make a convincing argument for the link between biodiversity and cultural diversity. "Pull back from the jargon," they caution, "and the essence is simple: Homogeneous landscapes—whether linguistic, cultural, biological, or genetic—are brittle and prone to failure." But a key point of failure in today's global design landscape lies precisely in the jargon: We need to invent new ways of writing, talking, and thinking about concepts of

_Q/_A Maria Popova Talks about Buzzword-Encrusted Language

You are writing for designers on DesignObserver.com. Is there a style or form that you use to reach this audience?

Not necessarily. One of the most wonderful and fascinating things about "designers"—and by that I mean the broad spectrum of people who practice, observe, write about, or are intrigued and inspired by any aspect of design culture—is that they tend to be very cross-disciplinarily curious, receptive, and willing to engage in just about any conversation, whatever medium or form it may come in.

This is a distinctly critical piece in which you attack "buzzword-encrusted language." What is this language and how do you avoid it?

The design world, especially the ever-growing piece of it that deals with the intersection of design and business, or creativity and corporation, tends to reduce complex arguments and ideas to sound bites that can fit on a Powerpoint slide. (Okay, perhaps Keynote.) Over the past few years—or, some might even say, decades—words and terms that once stood for something have become vacant of meaning, thrown around as weightless fluff. I've sat through countless conferences, presentations, panels, and other public forums where a speaker would machine-shoot buzzwords—"innovation," "design thinking," "systems design," "process not product," and so on—without contributing any original insight or, in many cases, without even rooting the respective term in a larger argument or case being made.

My philosophy is, if you have something of substance to say, you can say it in natural, honest language that doesn't sound like it came from a Malcolm Gladwell book title generator. Inside every business executive and creative director and journalist is a curious and creatively restless five-year-old; get that five-year-old excited about whatever you're arguing for and you'll get the grown-up to pay attention. But that won't happen with clunky and contrived buzz-speak.

You write that "The way we talk and write about these issues is incredibly important." How should writing about design be accomplished?

I don't believe in prescriptive one-size-fits-all approaches, especially when it comes to something like writing, which hinges on the…here's another buzzword, but it doesn't have to be…authenticity of the voice that's presenting the idea. So I can only speak for myself. I recall something I read in a philosophy book once; it was about the Buddha's advice on mindful speech, which has to answer to two simple criteria: Is it true, and is it helpful.

A lot of design criticism, and criticism in general, focuses all too heavily, solemnly even, on the former. It's much harder to critique and offer a solution than it is to just critique, and often much less immediately gratifying. When I write, I try to think about both—whatever I'm arguing has to always be true for me (because, in the end, there's no such thing as a grand capital Truth), and it has to, in some way, leave readers with something beyond the mere recognition of the problem—an idea, an insight, a direction of thought that might, just maybe, lead to a solution.

Do you find that you slip into jargon, simply because it is such a viable shorthand?

Oh, absolutely. We all do. Jargon is to writing and speaking what stereotypes are to thinking—mental schemata, shortcuts, which free up cognitive load in allowing us not to make the same mental computations and assessments every time we address the same problem. These shortcuts can be good (roaring lion usually means run because you're about to get eaten) or bad (racism, sexism, you-name-it-ism). But what's true of stereotypes is also true of jargon: In the end, no universal rule of thumb is an acceptable substitute for personal judgment and integrity. We do our best to express ourselves honestly and with conviction, and that's the most we can do. Sometimes jargon helps us do that, sometimes it hinders us, and the gift for telling the difference between the two is among the gifts, or perhaps arduously acquired skills, that set great writers apart from the rest.

What is the language that designers should speak in their writing?

A language of cultural curiosity and compassion but, above all, a language that's all their own. Who am I to prescribe that?

*Could it be that as soon as we lose our linguistic grasp
of a species, we stop talking about it, then thinking about it,
then caring about it?*

"humanitarian design"; we need new language that doesn't homogenize entire cultures, new vocabulary that better reflects the intricate lace of the world's biocultural and psychosocial diversity as a drawing board for design.

To borrow from science and resilience theory, the work of Italian anthropologist and linguist Luisa Maffi, founder of biocultural diversity conservancy Terralingua, offers ample evidence that the loss of indigenous languages is followed closely by a loss of biodiversity. Without trying to oversimplify what's clearly a complex issue, this raises an obvious question: Could it be that as soon as we lose our linguistic grasp of a species, we stop talking about it, then thinking about it, then caring about it? When it comes to humanitarian design, we never invented this language in the first place, a language that allows us to properly talk, think, and care about indigenous communities and their biocultural landscape. Our jargon has set us up for failure from the get-go.

So what can the design community do? I don't have the answer. And I am certain no one person does. But cross-disciplinary teams of designers, scientists, anthropologists, linguists, and writers might. Teams that include what GlobalVoices founder Ethan Zuckerman recently called "bridge figures"—people who have one foot in an expert community, be that technology or design or another discipline, and one in a local community benefiting from this expertise. For now, let's embrace our responsibility as designers and design writers to honor cultural diversity. Let's stop hiding behind industry jargon. Let's invent a new language that allows us to better think, talk, and care about indigenous cultures and microcommunities before we try to retrofit them to our projects and our preconceptions. Language that is just, because this is not just semantics. Above all, let's welcome voices and viewpoints from other disciplines, other parts of the world, and other paradigms. Enough with the industry panels already.

CASE STUDY:
FANZINES BY TEAL TRIGGS

ADRIAN SHAUGHNESSY

Designer, writer, broadcaster, and publisher of *Unit Editions*
(*Originally published in* The Wire #324, *February 2011*)

This book is a densely illustrated and sharply argued history of the humble fanzine. Written by Teal Triggs, a graphic design academic, it is a switchback ride through the outlaw terrain of samizdat zine publishing. Triggs shows how fanzines offer a maverick history of pop culture; how they have acted as pathfinders for stylistic and editorial developments in mainstream media; and how they presaged the DIY publishing revolution made possible by the internet.

Triggs is a surefooted guide: she maintains a cool analytical detachment and avoids tipping over into fannish obsession, or for that matter, academic turgidity. Her book begins by delving into the antecedents of zines. The term "fanzine" was coined by the American Sci-Fi enthusiast and zine producer Louis Russell Chauvenet in 1940 "when he declared his preference for the term 'fanzine' rather than 'fanmag.'" By 1949 the word had entered the cultural lexicon and appeared as an entry in the *Oxford English Dictionary*.

The author somewhat fancifully connects contemporary fanzines with publishing activity at the time of the French Revolution, Thomas Paine's pamphlet Common Sense (1776), and the engravings of William Blake (1778). She is, however, on more measurable ground when she links zines to the pamphleteering of Dada, Fluxus and the Situationists. From the publications of these avant-garde groups we can follow a lineage that travels through Sci-Fi "fan" mags of 1940s America, on through the Underground press of the 1960s, and finally arrives in the Xeroxed and stapled fanzines of the '70s and '80s.

If the punk eruption of the mid-'70s ushered in an era of DIY music and labels, then a generation of writers, designers and editors also seized the moment to bypass the publishing establishment and speak directly to like-minded audiences. Triggs stresses the importance of Jamie Reid's Suburban Press (1970–75)—"a Situationist-inspired publication that, along with *Sub* magazine and King Mob, provided a bridge between the hippie press and punk fanzines," and the appearance in 1976 of Mark Perry's *Sniffin' Glue*. She points out, however, that Perry rejected the "first fanzine" tag and cited Greg Shaw's *Who Put the Bomp* (1970–79) and Brian Hogg's *Bam Balam* (1974–c.1980s) as precursors.

It wasn't only music that fanned the fanzine revolution: oppositional political movements of all colours—anarcho-punks, skinheads and sexual revolutionaries—adopted the fanzine format to advance contrarian cultural agendas. Triggs devotes a chapter to the riot grrrl movement and its smart use of the fanzine format. She notes the radical subversion of feminine iconography—lipstick lettering, romance fiction, '50s housewives

'70s and '80s Fanzines
are the epitome of D.I.Y.,
some are photocopied
sheets, like *Starlet*, others
like *Letigre* and *Twinkle*
Eye are printed offset on
newsprint.

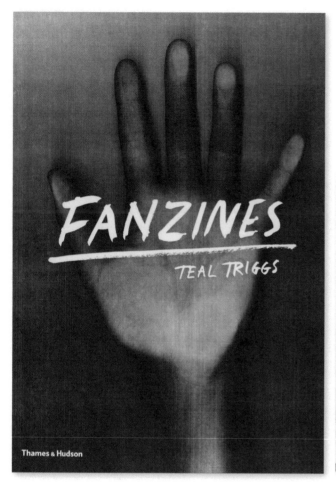

Cover of Fanzines by Teal Triggs represents the photocopy ethos of the zones.

Vague, *Kitten Carousel*, *Bombshell* and *Ablaze* care little for the niceties of design, but the emotional quality is clear.

with aprons—to sanction the ethos that "riot grrrls were both empowered to be feminists and had the choice to be feminine."

Triggs makes the point that not all fanzines were oppositional, and that the scene has always been big enough to accommodate football zines, comic zines and "a housewife from Virginia or from Hertfordshire producing a zine about collecting Pez dispensers." She also notes the existence of a burgeoning meta zine culture involving fanzines about fanzines, academic symposia and zine festivals.

Fanzine producers were early adopters of the internet. E-zines flourished around bulletin boards and the hacking and phreaking movements of the early '80s. But as vast swathes of the fanzine audience moved online—first to MySpace, then Facebook, and latterly Twitter—fanzine producers retained

their stubborn fondness for paper and printed formats. Triggs quotes one zine theorist who noted that the internet has made "communication too easy and that the deviant socialization process of the underground might be lost as a consequence." In the final chapter she identifies "craft" and "making by hand" as prime drivers in fanzine culture.

As a graphic designer in the 80s and 90s I was so bound up in learning the formal aspects of my craft—grids, the laws of typography and sophisticated production techniques—that I rarely felt much empathy with the seemingly chaotic and anti-formalist fanzine scene. Yet today, I look at the covers and spreads from early zines and I see a lost Eden: a graphic arcadia that has been submerged in a tidal wave of uniformity, visual conservatism, and the homogenizing effect of rampant commercialism.

Ⓠ/Ⓐ Adrian Shaughnessy Talks about Being Personal

What is the virtue of the funny/surprising anecdote?

Most graphic design is not autobiographical, in the way that painting and other forms of visual art often are. Therefore, to understand graphic designers we usually have to look at their actions and words rather than their work—ye shall know them by their anecdotes! An anecdote, if sharply observed and sharply told, can take us to the core of someone faster than historical analysis.

What do you feel are the advantages of using a strongly personal writing voice (as opposed to the more distant third-person one)?

My own preference is for something in between. It is a very rare writer who can impose him or herself into a piece of writing and not obscure their subject. Equally, I find overtly academic texts where the writer's personality has been eliminated, to be off-putting. When I started writing about design I scrupulously avoided the first person. Then I realized that I was usually writing about subjects that I had direct personal experience with, and it was this that gave my writing conviction. So I gradually allowed the personal pronoun to creep in. I still have to boot it out occasionally.

What role do you feel personal taste should play in design criticism?

I'd go as far as to say that I don't think there is any criticism without personal taste. Absolute objectivity is impossible. The art of critical writing, however, is to prove that your personal taste is correct—or at least valid. We like those critics who share our prejudices and give voice to them.

What do designers stand to gain through the honing of their writing skills?

Clarity. Mastery of their subject matter. A deeper understanding of the world. Heightened communication skills. I meet so many designers (mostly students) who have no interest in joining the conventional world of professional graphic design. They are part of what I have started to call "post-graphic design." This is a phrase I've been using to describe my teaching: It means that since it is no longer an attractive option to work in a traditional design studio or in the design department of a corporation, students are looking for alternative ways of making a living. And one of the ways they can do this is through taking ownership of their own projects. I see students interested in using design skills not to make beautiful design objects and statutes (which I wanted to do), but to use their skills to achieve social and cultural goals. Almost certainly, this will involve "reporting skills"—and that means writing skills.

Being a designer informs your writing; does being a writer inform your design?

Yes, mainly in the increased understanding of a subject I have after writing about it, but also in quite mundane ways. For instance, I am never shy about suggesting copy changes to clients when I see that the copy they have given me is bad—or doesn't fit into my layouts. For a long time I suffered silently while trying to get bad copy to fit. Then I developed the confidence to suggest better copy, and as a result, my design has often been "improved" simply by rewriting the copy to make it fit. You can't always do this—I wouldn't try rewriting a legal document, for example—but it can benefit design and communication if designers are able to suggest copy improvements.

CASE STUDY:
THOMAS LENTHAL:
The Deejay of Visual References

VERONIQUE VIENNE

Freelance author of more than a dozen books
(*Originally published in* Eye *magazine #73, Autumn 2009*)

French luxury brands are not for the faint of heart. Their ad campaigns can test the sensibility of those among us who are not sexually aroused by the sight of action-figure goddesses in torn fishnet stockings. In the last decade, as the result of an unholy alliance between the couture world and the contemporary art scene (thanks to French billionaire and collector Bernard Arnault, chairman and CEO of LVMH), trollop chic and hard-core glamour have become the mainstay of many upscale fashion magazines. Luxury, once synonymous with opulence, has become a guerrilla tactic against sanitized bourgeois values. French creative director Thomas Lenthal can be credited for setting the standards for this strange phenomenon. His 2001 campaign for Dior is nothing short of a porn-hip manifesto.

An [alumnus] of French *Glamour*, a founding partner of slick fashion magazine *Numéro*, and a seasoned freelance advertising art director with clients like Cacharel, Tod's, and Kenzo, Lenthal had been hired by John Galliano, Dior's new sibyl, to "wake up sleeping beauty"—to turn the then-sluggish couture brand into an avant-garde sensation. He directed UK photographer Nick Knight to stage a series of tableaux that looked, at first glance, like police pictures of injured car crash survivors, their bruised bodies covered with diesel fuel, their clothes a mess, the dazed expression on their faces evidence of their bewildered state of mind. The women in the photographs, swathed in skimpy yet extravagant togs, sported strappy high-heel sandals and clutched pristine Dior handbags.

The campaign put Dior on the map. "It was meant to be outrageously contemporary," says Lenthal. "Galliano had asked

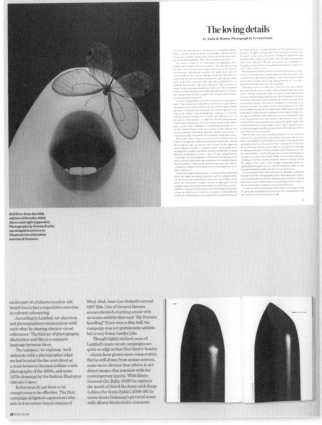

↑ Spread from *Eye* magazine *#73*

us to *please, do burn down the house,* so we did." However, what seemed to most an unnecessarily obscene proclamation on the part of what had been until now a very boudoir-ish brand, was in fact a superlative exercise in cultural referencing. "Art directors and photographers communicate with each other by sharing obscure visual references," says Lenthal. He explains how the history of photography, illustration, and film is a common language between them. "For instance, I'd describe to a photographer what I have in mind for the next shoot as a cross between German lesbian erotic photographs of the 1930s and 1970 drawings by fashion illustrator Antonio Lopez."

References do not have to be conspicuous to be effective. The Spring 2001 Dior campaign, particularly gruesome in the wake of the September 11 carnage, had originally delighted cognoscenti who saw in it an astute visual citation of *Week-End*, the surreal 1967 film by Jean-Luc Godard in which actors are involved in a series of grisly car crashes. One of the most famous scenes showed a burning wreck with an ironic subtitle that read "My Hermès handbag!" If you were a film buff, as many Frenchmen were and still are, the campaign was perceived not as a gratuitously sadistic gesture, but as a very funny insider's joke.

"Put a short caption under a picture, and suddenly it has a lot to say."

Though highly stylized, none of Lenthal's most recent campaigns for luxury brands manage to be quite as edgy as the 2001 Dior visual fender-bender. Clients have grown more conservative these days. Still, he draws from arcane sources, some more obvious than others, to art-direct images that resonate with the contemporary psyche. With Mario Sorrenti (for Bally) he explores the world of David Hockney; with Serge Leblon (for Sonia Rykiel) he mixes Sonia Delaunay's pictorial sense with Alexey Brodovitch's cinematic editing; with Mert Alas and Marcus Piggott (for YSL's Opium) he mocks naturalism, preferring instead the meta-universe of plastic surgery; with Sølve Sundsbø (for Yves Saint Laurent Parfums) he takes off on Man Ray; with Inez van Lamsweerde and Vinoodh Matadin (for Dior Joaillerie) he pays homage to photographers Serge Lutens and Hiro.

His most intriguing [collaboration] is probably with Juergen Teller, the new enfant terrible of fashion photography (Teller is the genius behind the provocative Marc Jacobs ad campaign featuring candid shots of trendy celebrities). "With less photo equipment than a German tourist, Juergen takes pictures that are incredibly lively," says Lenthal. However, referencing is a game Teller plays reluctantly. Case in point: the campaign he shot with Lenthal for Yves Saint Laurent,

Thomas Lenthal
'Art directors and photographers communicate with each other by sharing obscure visual references.'

French luxury brands are not for the faint of heart, *writes Véronique Vienne.* Their ad campaigns can test the sensibility of those who are not aroused by the sight of action-figure goddesses in torn fishnet stockings. In the past decade, as the result of an unholy alliance between the couture world and the contemporary art scene (thanks in no small part to Bernard Arnault, billionaire collector and chairman of the fashion conglomerate LVMH), trollop chic and hardcore glamour have become the mainstay of many upscale fashion magazines. Luxury, once synonymous

with opulence, has become a guerrilla attack on sanitised bourgeois values.

It was French creative director Thomas Lenthal who set the standards with a 2001 campaign for Dior that was nothing short of a porn-hip manifesto.

An alumnus of French *Glamour*, a founding partner of slick fashion magazine *Numéro* and a seasoned freelance advertising art director with clients such as Cacharel, Tod's and Kenzo, Lenthal was hired by Dior designer John Galliano to 'wake up sleeping beauty'. He directed British photographer Nick Knight to stage a

series of tableaux that looked at first glance like police pictures of injured car crash survivors, their bruised bodies covered with diesel, their clothes a mess, dazed expressions on their faces. The models, swathed in skimpy yet extravagant togs, sported strappy high-heeled sandals and clutched pristine Dior handbags.

The campaign put Dior on the map. 'It was meant to be outrageous,' says Lenthal. 'The client said, "Please, do burn down the house," so we did.' However, what seemed to most an unnecessarily obscene proclamation

ART AND ART DIRECTION

↑ *Eye's* design is a neutral frame for the work being showcased.

in which models on stilettos were dangerously propped on ledges, high on the rooftops of the Paris Opéra Garnier. The photographs spoof rather than celebrate the *Cat on a Hot Tin Roof* motif. Charming parodies, they are unretouched evidence that the age of irony may, at long last, have run its course.

Likewise, Lenthal begins to show signs of being tired of running circles around smart cultural references. In 2006, he launched a stylish, soft-core magazine, *Paradis*, with two separate French and English editions, to which he invites his friends to contribute. There is no girlie centerfold, but the magazine will typically feature a 60-page erotic portfolio by Teller. It's the old *Playboy* formula: photographs of pretty women in various stages of undress are sandwiched in between celebrity interviews (by famed critic Hans-Ulrich Obrist), investigative pieces, behind-the-scenes reportages, and visual essays by still-life photographers Erwan Frotin and Guido Mocafico, with whom Lenthal collaborates on Dior jewelry campaigns. The notable presence of still-life photography in Paradis is a reflection of Lenthal's growing interest for less spectacular forms of provocation. Recently, he is developing a growing interest [in] quaint 19th century portraiture and black-and-white journalistic reportages.

As an art director, Lenthal runs his fashion campaigns the same way a deejay runs a show, mixing and matching visual codes as if they were samples or musical genres. Yet as an editor, he finds that concentrating on one picture at a time is just as stimulating. "Photography is an incredibly potent medium," he says. "Put a short caption under a picture, and suddenly it has a lot to say."

ⓠ/ⓐ Veronique Vienne Talks about Her Handicaps

You started as an art director. Why did you switch to writing?

I wanted my byline on the page. Art directors don't sign their work— their name is buried on the masthead. Writers make a lot less money than art directors (about one-tenth!), but they stand proudly behind their work.

How did you learn to write?

By reading John McPhee, Joan Didion, Mary McCarthy, Gustave Flaubert—and *Harper's* magazine.

How did you develop a writing style?

Being French was a serious handicap. To sound American, I had to learn to write short sentences, with no more than one subordinate clause. Also, I had to learn to put the subjects and the verbs in the front of my sentences. In French, they trail at the end of sentences. Call it delayed gratification. In my native language, the payoff comes last!

You write a lot about design. What triggers the subjects you take on?

I wanted to share with colleagues and friends what I loved about the field of design. It turned out that very few people I knew bothered to read what I wrote. It's always a surprise to find out that I have readers out there.

Do you write for designers or for a mass audience?

Before writing about design (an elite activity, I admit), I wrote first-person pieces for newspapers and magazines. I wrote short essays about "French" topics: how to make a quiche, tie a scarf, kiss a man, lose weight while eating bonbons, visit Paris, decorate a boudoir, cook with butter, make an entrance, buy lingerie, have an affair—and age gracefully. I wrote a bestseller called *The Art of Doing Nothing*. What else do you expect from someone who comes from a country where people enjoy seven-week paid vacations?

How do you distinguish, if at all, journalism from criticism?

Journalism is linear. Art criticism is an arc. It completes a circle.

What are your favorite themes?

I like to write about graphic design because no one knows what it is all about. (I define graphic design as an assemblage of signs that makes one feel intelligent.)

CASE STUDY:

MY ANNOTATED INTERVIEW WITH MIKE SALISBURY

 MICHAEL DOOLY

Michael Dooley is a designer, educator, and *Print* contibuting editor.
In this interview, Dooley takes the reader through the interview process

Mike Salisbury created Joe Camel in 1987. Four years later the American Medical Association reported that six year olds could identify Camel's character better than Mickey Mouse, Fred Flintstone, Bugs Bunny, or Barbie. And in 1996, *Print* magazine hired me to interview Mike about the cigarette campaign he created, which was still going strong.

I have strong feelings about cigarettes. My mother had died from lung cancer when I was 17 years old. But in my role as objective reporter, I decided at the outset to stay impersonal. The only exception was my end tag bio; playing off a well-known Bill Clinton quote at the time, I wrote that I "never inhaled tobacco."

I met Mike for the first time when we sat down for dinner at Gordon Biersch, a brewery/restaurant in Pasadena. I can't resist a pun, no matter how bad, so when Mike ordered the ribeye I immediately told the waiter I'd have the same, just in case I wanted to title the piece "My Steak with Salisbury." Instead, my editor wisely settled on "Defending Joe Camel, Sort of."

Our meal lasted a leisurely four hours, which apparently isn't the norm. While conducting an even lengthier interview with Rudy VanderLans at his studio for *Print* in 1992, he remarked that when Patrick Coyne was writing his Emigre feature for *Communication Arts*, he was in and out within a half hour.

The following is the full transcript from the July/August 1996 issue of *Print*. I've also added my commentary.

Since career summaries tend to resemble laundry lists, which can often be tedious, I made Mike's as brief as possible. And to connect with younger designers, I began my intro by linking Mike to a more easily recognizable name. The David Carson connection first occurred to me because I knew that he'd, umm, "adapted" Mike's 1985 *To Live and Die in L.A.* movie poster two years later, for a *Transworld Skateboarding* cover.

He's an avid surfer who began his career designing a surf magazine and gained notoriety with his radically experimental covers and spreads for lifestyle and rock-'n'-roll publications. No, it's not who you think; it's Mike Salisbury, who was creating a sensation with West *back when David Carson was only a teenager. Salisbury went on to art direct* City *and* Rolling Stone *and design hundreds of movie campaigns, including* Raiders of the Lost Ark, Jurassic Park, *and* Aliens. *His client list includes Levi-Staruss, Michael Jackson, and Disneyland. Salisbury's latest design effort, a cyber-sleaze porno mag called* Rage, *{Hustler's Larry Flynt, editor} should also provoke some rage, at least among feminists and fans of refined design. I recently got together with the original Southern California bad-boy*

↑ *Joe Camel*, the venerable Camel cigarette mascot, received a make-over to appeal to a younger audience. The campaign was a success and the outcry against it was also.

art director for an unfiltered discussion about his controversial creation, Joe Camel.

I found Mike to be a delightfully entertaining raconteur. His design career dates back to the early 1960s, and his life is jam-packed with amazing adventures and significant accomplishments. I could have easily built a full feature profile from our conversation, but I'd only been allocated one page spread. And so, when trimming my text I kept a tight focus on a single topic. I'm also most grateful to my *Print* editors, Carol Stevens and Julie Lasky.

Keeping the magazine's readership in mind, I put a design-related comment up front

DOOLEY: When you and Scott Mednick debated the morality of cigarette advertising at the '93 AIGA conference he claimed that, since you said you were willing to promote anything legal, by extension that could include Hitler.
SALISBURY: That's a cheap shot, an easy shot, but it's not a fair analogy. Cigarettes and the Nazi party don't have anything in common. You should compare what I do with what the movie industry does with product placement instead. Ask Oliver Stone why everybody in *Natural Born Killers* was smoking, and does he think it influences people, and is it an unfair, subliminal influence.

Next I moved on to specifics.

DOOLEY: Did Camel choose you for your reputation for reaching the youth market?
Salisbury: They came to me because of all the movie work and nostalgic, retro advertising I've done. The original concept was to reprise old motion picture posters and have heroes like Humphrey Bogart and Gary Cooper smoking Camels, but it bombed because the target audience doesn't know or care about old movies. Then we put a camel's head on Sam Spade and they still didn't understand it. But when we gave him the *Miami Vice* look, it got great test response, and that became the campaign.

Camel later ran a campaign with a "Pleasure to Burn" tagline, in the mid-2000s. It used a pulp detective-style character wearing a period trench coat and fedora. It also closely resembled Mike's early, retro drawings. When I showed it to him recently he just shrugged and told me that's how the ad game is played.

Next, I took advantage of Mike's *Miami Vice* comment as an opportunity to hit the subliminal snout issue.

DOOLEY: That raises a side issue: some people claim Joe Camel is a phallic symbol. Were you really thinking of Don Johnson's johnson? [See: I can't stop myself.]
SALISBURY: I never thought of that until some lady called me and said, "Isn't that like a dick?" I was just trying to make this stupid head have some kind of expression I could change from ad to ad, and I remembered how Sean Connery as James Bond could move his eyebrows so expressively. So I ripped off his eyes and eyebrows and Don Johnson's hair.

I assume readers hate being bogged down with numbers as much as I do. So rather than cite specifics statistics I tossed out a generality that worked just as well.

DOOLEY: Besides women, kids are the only way for the tobacco industry to expand its market, and Camel's share among teenagers has been rising astronomically.
SALISBURY: Camel wasn't going after new smokers; they were trying to get smokers to switch. They felt their target market was a guy about 25, who had a truck and a T-shirt job.

Mike's response was a dodge. But rather than press the matter directly, I decided to approach it from another angle. The fact that it worked surprised me. I was also grateful for Mike's magnanimity.

DOOLEY: But couldn't a campaign directed at pickup drivers appeal just as well to adolescants who want to feel more confident, improve their image, be more popular?
SALISBURY: Now that's a better, more reasonable argument than comparing cigarettes to Hitler. What you're saying is

There's an old adage that says to save your toughest question, the one you're not sure what the reaction will be, until the end. That way, if your interviewee is insulted enough to cut the conversation short, you'll still have accumulated plenty of material.

probably right. If this kid identifies with what's targeted to another, older guy, I agree it will have an influence.

You're right, I sold a lot of cigarettes: sales went from $30 million a year to $330 million. I'd like to take all the credit, but advertising doesn't encourage smoking, it encourages brand loyalty.

I'll tell you the real reason kids smoke. They know it's bad for them but they see the guys in Guns 'n' Roses [yes, it was 1996], and Madonna and all their heroes in movies and music videos smoking. I remember seeing James Dean smoke in movies and thinking that was cool, and I don't think I was aware of cigarette advertising.

It's also a way they can rebel and piss off their parents. Their parents aren't going to smoke, they're all vegetarians and New-Agers.

And kids will choose Camel because it's not their father's brand: it's not Marlboro. And maybe they're also more aware of Camel because of what I did.

Our conversation had been easygoing throughout, but at this point I felt even more comfortable. I continued to press the issue.

DOOLEY: But Joe Camel is as much an icon as Madonna: Each can contribute subliminally to the behavior of an insecure adolescent.
SALISBURY: You're right, I'm probably responsible, guilty as charged. If advertising, product placement, manufacture,

sales, and government subsidies encourage people to smoke, then I'm part of that whole machinery.

Again, I was surprised. This time it was because it seemed that, in the campaign's nine years, Mike was confronting, and even conceding, on this issue for the first time. My next question was meant to raise the human equation.

Dooley: Do you feel any responsibility about what you advertise?
SALISBURY: I figure the people who smoke have made their own decision. I feel a responsibility to myself. I think about whether I should be a part of something I wouldn't encourage my own kids to do. I actually turned the job down at first. But they kept coming back and I got caught up in doing it as a problem-solving exercise, and that probably took over the morality issue at some point, like the accelerator of a jet plane.

In all honesty, I really didn't think I'd be good at selling cigarettes. I didn't think we could knock Marlboro out.

I regularly use Mike's answer to introduce an ethics discussion with my design history students. It also works as a lead-in to Tibor Kalman's "First Things First" manifesto of 1999.

There's an old adage that says to save your toughest question, the one you're not sure what the reaction will be, until the end. That way, if your interviewee is insulted enough to cut the conversation short, you'll still have accumulated plenty

*If I'm not learning what I have to say,
and how to say it, as part of my process,
then what's the point?*

Q/A Michael Dooley on Discovery and Skepticism

You are a designer and art director, what prompted you to start writing?

C'mon, Steve: I can't let you have all the fun. But seriously. I'd been a design instructor in the 1980s. I loved teaching.... still do.... and I thought about how I could also educate to a wider audience through my writing. My lifelong interest in comic books and cartoons led me to *Fantagraphics*, publishers of *The Comics Journal*. TCJ is a smart, independent magazine that has been covering the medium with in-depth news, reviews, and interviews since 1976.

Eventually, I decided I wanted to jump from my favorite comics publication to my favorite design magazine. So in 1990 I sent tearsheets of my writing to *Print*, and in my cover letter I asked if I could review the catalog for "High & Low," the MoMA exhibition that dealt with the relationship between modern art and aspects of popular culture such as caricature, graffiti, advertising, and comics. The editor, Carol Stevens, wrote back to say that she wanted me to critique not only the book, but the entire exhibit as well. Well, of course. And so I flew from Los Angeles to New York to see the show. And Marty Fox, *Print's* editor-in-chief, soon added my name to the masthead as contributing editor, much to my pride and delight.

What was your first assignment and what did it teach you?

The main lesson of my "High and Low" feature, one that I'd already begun to learn at *The Comics Journal*, is to approach writing as a design process. I never had any formal education as a professional writer. So I simply apply the modernist design principles I'd picked up during my student days at Pratt Institute: Structure, simplify, etc. It was only later, after talking with professionals, that I was told I'd been doing it "wrong," and that the most efficient and expedient method is to first decide what you're going to say at the outset, then draw up an outline, then gather and slot your information, and bang, you're done.

Thus informed, I decided I didn't want to write the "correct" way.... still don't, never will. Sure, my method takes a lot more time; I rewrite much more than I write. But still, I much prefer to have my story evolve organically from investigating the assignment instead of simply inserting information into pre-established templates, Mad Libs style.

[Type designer] Jeff Keedy once told me that he only writes to annoy people; otherwise, what's the point? Well, my take is this: If I'm not learning what I have to say, and how to say it, as part of my process, then

what's the point? And where's the fun? The adventure? For me discovery, not assembly, is where the action is.

You're writing contains a certain skepticism. Is that your voice?

Oh, yeah. I think it's important.... essential, even, for writers to maintain a healthy skepticism. Otherwise, you're just a note-taker. I've been a skeptic since I was seven. That's when I was fortunate enough to discover Harvey Kurtzman's *Mad* comic books, which lampooned much of the culture of the 1950s. Most important was Harvey's masterworks, the Goodman Beaver stories in *Help!* magazine, astutely observed morality tales superbly rendered by Will Elder. But I'm not a cynic. What I also learned from those comics was an acute sense of absurdity. In fact, my cosmic worldview can be summed up in three words: it's all funny.

Do you think of yourself as a journalist or an observer?

Yes. Oh, you want more? Well, when I'm conducting interviews and writing profiles, I consider myself a reporter, and do my best to abide by journalistic standards. For opinion pieces and essays, ideally I'm an observer, and a researcher, and an explorer. But most of the time both practices overlap. And that's always enjoyable.

What is the most satisfying aspect of writing about design?

The money? Hah! But seriously, though.... Besides discovering and learning, I also love sharing. And not only with readers. I bring my newfound knowledge to my students on a constant basis. Plus, I'm very gratified when my work is picked up in outlets beyond the design publication "ghetto." It indicates that the general public may share an interest in design, and that I may be writing generously enough to speak to them. And how many other jobs exist where, if you want to connect with people, all you have to do is decide to write a story on them.

I know, that's several "most satisfying" answers. Hey, I'm not a mathematician. I'm a writer. And yeah, a designer.

9 mg. "tar", 0.6 mg. nicotine av. per cigarette by FTC method.

HOLLYWOOD

CAMEL LIGHTS

LOW TAR CAMEL TASTE·

Smooth character.

SURGEON GENERAL'S WARNING: SMOKING CAUSES LUNG CANCER, HEART DISEASE, AND EMPHYSEMA.

↑ *The Smooth Character* lit flames under the smoking and anti-smoking factions in the United States.

of material. But by this point I wasn't worried. I was confident that Mike would respond to anything I tossed his way. So, ahem.

Dooley: With all the subtle and sophisticated design work you've done over the past 30 years, does it bother you that your current notoriety is based on such a schlocky, hackneyed concept?

SALISBURY: That's a very perceptive insight; you're absolutely right. That's probably much more important than the morality question: how I personally feel about being known for this piece of crap that people think is great advertising. It's a pretty shitty piece of art.

I didn't want to do it that way. I would have done something realistic but the marketing and testing and everything said they should use airbrush and bright colors. So I told them I could do it better than anybody.

We could have just flatout illustrated a dumb camel with Rapidograph outline and an airbrush and it wouldn't have worked. But I styled the guy, I gave him personality, I gave him situations, I gave him dimension. I was up day and night for months. And we billed more than I ever billed in my life.

I did my job and made a lot of money. But was it the right job to do morally? I don't really know the answer.

I haven't sold guns yet.

When conducting Q&As I try to come across more as an explorer than as a blatant propagandist. I'd prefer to let the readers make up their own minds, based on the texts. So after the interview ran I was pleased to receive favorable feedback from both sides of the debate. Opponents of Joe Camel congratulated me for having "exposed" Mike. And Mike congratulated me for putting together what he felt was a terrific piece.

A year after the interview ran, R.J. Reynolds retired the campaign. And I took the opportunity to write an opinion piece for the *AIGA* Journal about new restrictions that had recently been placed on cigarette advertising. To keep it from reading like a lecture I turned my commentary into the form of a barroom dialogue between Old Joe and the Marlboro Man. Mike and I continue to keep in touch. Most recently, he's been a guest speaker at my class.

One last comment. When I listen to other interviews, I'm amazed—and often frustrated—at how frequently interviewers either interrupt the conversation or jump to their next question at any slight pause. But I always like to assume that the interviewees may have more to say upon reflection, as Mike did with his last line. And that may be the best advice I can give when talking with people: shut up and listen.

WRITING WITH IMAGES

WRITING DESIGN

VERBAL

VISUAL

Writing is design and design is writing. Admittedly, that is a rhythmic sound bite, and there are exceptions to the rule. Yet increasingly, designers (and artists) are using text in their design and artwork. Graphic design has always been a mix of word and picture, but currently, text type or text as image is employed as a form of both personal and universal expression. This sampler of simple and intricate uses of words, sayings, and statements is indicative of how reading, writing, and research are being redefined in an increasingly media-saturated verbal and visual culture.

CASE STUDY:

THE NOSE

SEYMOUR CHWAST

From the coeditor of the famous *Push Pin Graphic*, this series of booklets on specific themes is both a showcase for Seymour Chwast's illustrations and a vehicle for expressing himself on political and cultural issues large and small.

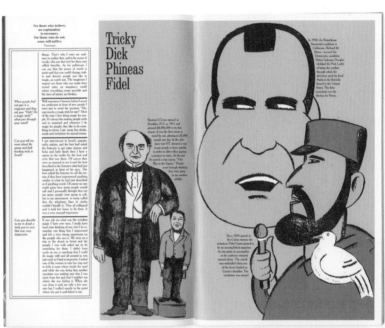

Another pet theme for *The Nose* was magic and tricks. Chwast assigned himself visual problems, like the Trojan horse (right), to solve related to the notion of illusion, and interpreted the ideas through his drawing and writing.

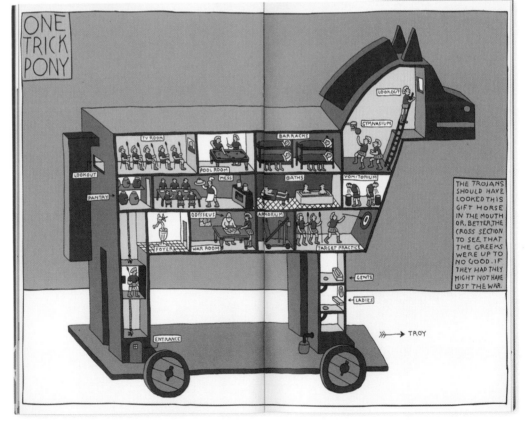

The Nose enabled Seymour Chwast to write, draw, and design on any subject of his choosing, from the theme of letter writing (opposite page) to the issue of "isms."

← Every opportunity to play with pictorial and verbal language was explored, including the cover (right) with the topsy-turvy head.

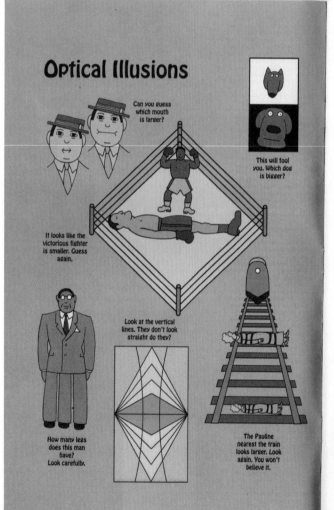

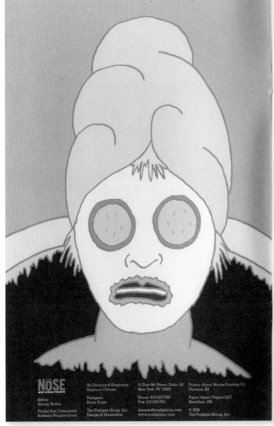

UNREAL

So much of what we consume every day is so unreal that reality has little meaning anymore. Remember when seeing was believing? Once, what we saw is what we got – truth was unassailable. No longer! Those were the good old, simple, halcyon, golden, honest days. Then reality was questioned. Bob Dylan wrote: "Are the birds really free from the chains of the skyway?" And that poetic question challenges all our assumptions of what is real today. If birds flying through the cage-less open air are not really free, then what truly are they? What is their reality? Is everything just illusion? • We accept too much unreality without question. Isn't that what advertising has fed us for all these years? Whether commercial or political isn't spin about creating an alternative reality? And isn't that what most entertainment is all about – making the unreal seem real—thanks to special effects. Even sports have devolved into a kind of fantasy. Athletes on steroids, despite recent senate investigations, get away with murder because the fact is they can really run faster, jump higher, hit further, and that's what we want to see! They are real, but simulated (and stimulated) through chemistry. Just because a woman or man has had been nipped and tucked to enhance their natural beauty doesn't mean they are less real than naturally beautiful women or men. Does it? They are as real as we want them or need them to be. • Reality is relative. . . but relative to what and who? If we want something to be, then we make it up. If we see ourselves as something unreal, then we become that something. And science (and technology) have become the enablers. • But don't forget this sobering reality: In the twenty first century the word "unreal" is a positive designation. "Wow, that's unreal!" is one of the highest compliments in the contemporary vernacular. Unreal is not synonymous with untrue (or lie). It simply means in most cases, over-the-top, under-the-radar, ahead-of-the-curve. If you must know, unreal is the new real—really. —Steven Heller

Unreal was rooted in Chwast's sense of the absurd in life. What is unreal is often very real. In this issue he assembles all the truths that appear implausible.

NOSE SEVENTEEN

Editor: Steven Heller

Production Consultant: Barbara Vaughn-Davis

Art Director & Illustrator: Seymour Chwast

Designer: Brian Ponto

55 East 9th Street, Suite 1G New York, NY 10003

Phone: 212.529.7590 Fax: 212.529.7631

thenose@pushpininc.com www.pushpininc.com

Printer: Steve Woods Printing Co. Phoenix, AZ

Paper: Smart Papers LLC Hamilton, OH

© 2006 The Pushpin Group, Inc.

The Pushpin Group, Inc. Design & Illustration

Where a blood relation sobs, an intimate friend should choke up, a distant acquaintance should sigh, a stranger should mearly fumble sympathetically with his handkerchief. —Mark Twain

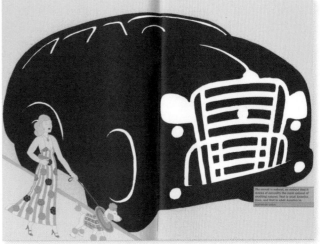

The unreal is natural, so natural that it makes of unreality the most natural of anything natural. This is what America does, and that is what America is. —Gertrude Stein

A specific editorial was written for *What Can We Say About Isms* by Steven Heller. The majority of additional texts were compiled and excerpted by Chwast, who then illustrated them in a variety of styles.

What Can We Say

Isms. There are simply too many of them. From agnosticism to zoism. With so many to choose from where does one find perfectionism in such obscurantism? How can we practice solipsism amid such fatalism? Is it possible to have a single encompassing ism that embraces all other isms? Or is it impossible to attain truism in a web of false isms? The answer is as plain as the nose on our respective faces. *Noseism* is a little known theory extolling optimism and absolutism. *Noseism*, which is often characterized by paroxysms of euphoria in its adherents (which may be sometimes construed as sexism because of its overt machoism), is a philosophical construct that imposes a certain abstract universalism, though sometimes relativism, on the world's varied isms rejecting positivism, also referred to as negativism. Racism is also rejected for good reasonism, having nothing to do with masochism but all to do with humanism. Yet for those without philosophical pluralism, the aim of *Noseism* is to impart an alternativism that relies entirely on plagiarism to build a body of intellectualism. Sarcasm (which is not an ism, but could be if it were sarcasmism) is not at the core of *Noseism*. Rather *Noseism* (not to be confused with noism which is the study of "no" or no-ledge) is a method of challenging the complexities of a complex world through deductive reasoning, from general to specific, also known as a syllogism, from occurring. Such is today's pessimism! *Noseism* is the grandest of all isms, and this issue, while rejecting Marxism, Volkism, and Stalinism, is an attempt to catalog and explain isms as we know them.—Steven Heller

About Isms?

NŌSE

Number 14
©2006 The Pushpin Group, Inc.

Editor
Steven Heller

Art Director & Illustrator
Seymour Chwast

Designer
Michi L. Turner

Ultratype fonts by
Seymour Chwast

The Pushpin Group, Inc.
Design and Illustration
56 East 9 Street
New York, NY 10003

Tel: 212. 529. 3590
Fax: 212.529.7631

thenose@pushpininc.com
www.pushpininc.com

Printer
Steve Woods Printing Co.
Phoenix, AZ

Paper
Sappi Fine Paper
Boston, Ma

CASE STUDY:
THINGS HE HAS LEARNED

STEFAN SAGMEISTER

Referencing, in part, the early twentieth-century progressive modernist typography parlant (type that metaphorically illustrates its literal meaning) and quoting the late twentieth century conceptually enigmatic, declarative typographies by Jenny Holzer, Barbara Kruger, Lawrence Weiner, and Ed Ruscha, Stefan Sagmeister's environmental typographic work bridges various media formats and materials. He is as comfortable with twigs and pipe as he is with ink and pixels. While his typography is associated with what might be termed the "epigram school" of art, it is not just regurgitating the other exemplars' methods but seeking out a new language while acknowledging existing languages.

His best-known collection of word-images, *Things I Have Learned in My Life So Far*, comes largely from a lengthy list of revelations jotted in his diary. Although each could be mistaken for self-help maxims (like "Trying to look good limits my life" and "Being not truthful works against me"), they nonetheless transcend being simplistic bromides by virtue of his series of interpretative typographic sculptures, which have come to characterize Sagmeister's hybrid output. Constructing words from such diverse objects as flowers, cacti, branches, sausages, toys, and toilet paper, not to mention the quirkier hair, semen, pollen, and intestines, the individual pieces run the gamut from what might be described as sublimely overt to lyrically ambiguous—yet never so abstract or arcane that an average viewer cannot somehow decipher each word leading to the message. One thing he rarely does is allow his words to be made into ham-fisted metaphors: For example, Sagmeister wisely did not compose "Everything I do always comes back to me" in a circle, for that would have been too obvious.

These are dividing spaces, each opening a new chapter in the magazine. Each month the magazine commissions another studio/artist with the design.

Studio: Sagmeister Inc.
Art Direction: Stefan Sagmeister
Design: Traian Stanescu
Photo: Oliver Meckes and Nicole Ottawa
Client: *.copy* magazine (Austria)
Year: 2005
Size: 9" × 11.5" (230 × 295 mm)

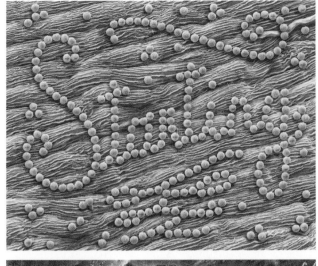

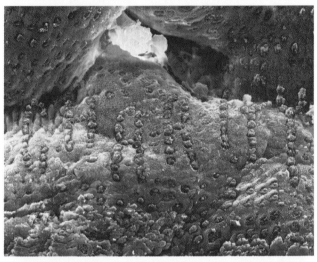

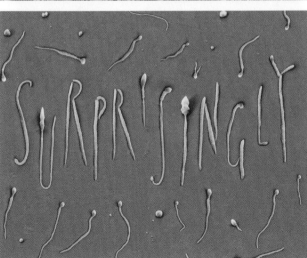
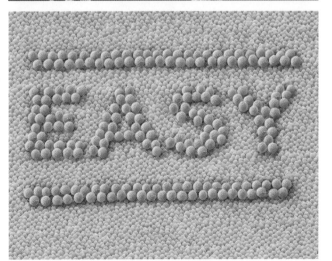

"We created the saying for the O.K. Zentrum in Linz," says Sagmeister. "Austrian school kids built the maxim out of 25,000 black and 35,000 white cloth hangers. Four hangers were bound together with wire fasteners to form a square; six of these completed squares formed a cube; and the cubes in turn formed pixels, creating the typography. Each letter stands about 10 feet (3 meters) high, with the entire sentence configuring a 125 foot (38 meter)-long block, a lacy typographic sculpture placed parallel to the building's façade on the Spittelwiese, a pedestrian zone in the center of Linz."

Concept: Stefan Sagmeister
Design: Stefan Sagmeister, Matthias Ernstberger, Craig Toomey, Brian Toomey
Curator: Martin Sturm, Paolo Bianchi
Coordination: Michael Weingartner, Rainer Jessl
Construction: Aron Rynda
Permits: Norbert Schweitzer
Production: Anet Sirna-Bruder
Documentary Photography: Otto Saxinger
Client: OK Zentrum Linz, Linz 2009, Linzer City Ring
Year: 2007
Size: 60,000 plastic hangers, 147'8" × 10' × 3'3" (45 × 3 × 1 m)

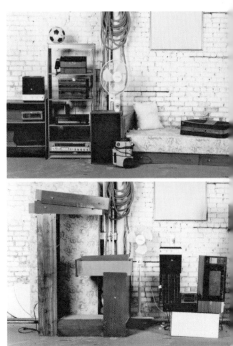

Six newly commissioned two-page spreads for the Austrian magazine *.copy*. Together they read: Having / guts / always / works out / for / me.

Design: Sagmeister Inc./Bela Borsodi
Art Direction: Stefan Sagmeister
Design: Matthias Ernstberger, Miao Wang, Stefan Sagmeister
Photo: Bela Borsodi.
Client: *.copy* magazine (Austria)
Year: 2003
Size: 9" × 11.5" (230 × 295 mm)

CASE STUDY:
344 QUESTIONS

▶▶▶ **STEFAN BUCHER**

344 Questions began with a column Stefan Bucher wrote and illustrated titled "ink & circumstance" for *Step inside design* magazine. The intention was to air aspects of design and illustration that Bucher believed were ignored in design discourse—the emotional side of the business and of the work itself. He admits that the column was "me standing on the porch, shooting off my mouth. Muttering, grumbling, ranting. I didn't know if anybody else cared about this stuff, or if I was alone in my opinions." Hence, he made the format of this handwritten column as engaging as possible—"to lure you in, and to give you something to enjoy even if you thought I was completely off base with my argument."

In his first book, *All Access*, Bucher had started a process of questioning what it means to be a designer. His second book, *344 Questions,* was a way to put it all together as helpful notions and countertop wisdom aimed at creative people who are trying to figure out their lives. The book is indeed small enough to carry everywhere, and since it costs less than $10, "you don't have to worry about messing it up," he insists. "In fact, it'll look better messed up than clean."

Some of the questions are arranged to build little rhythms, but for the most part, Bucher wanted the book to feel like a candid conversation. "As an immigrant I sometimes go overboard with the language, trying to show off. I worked hard not to do that here. It would've been malapropos, ungermane—deleterious even!"

Bucher says he is a hermit and a crank, "so thoughts are constantly swirling around my head." Every other month, he would just write about the thing that was most on his mind. In terms of both the writing and the illustration, making "ink & circumstance" and then *344 Questions* was "like holding a stick into a cotton candy maker."

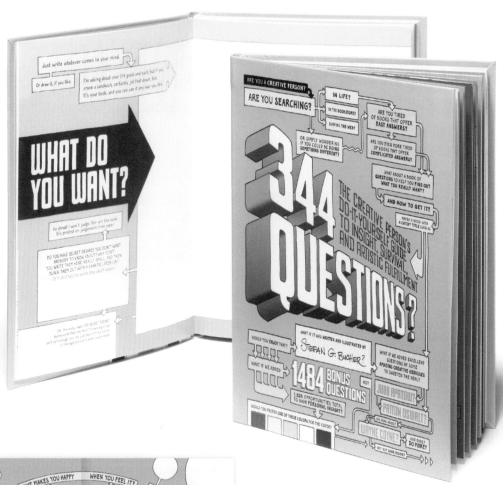

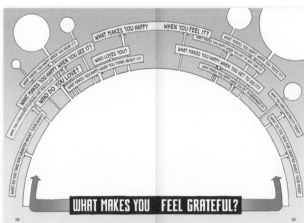

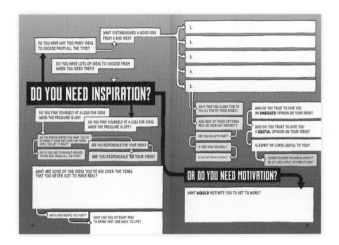

344 Questions:
Various pages,
designed and written
by Stefan Bucher.

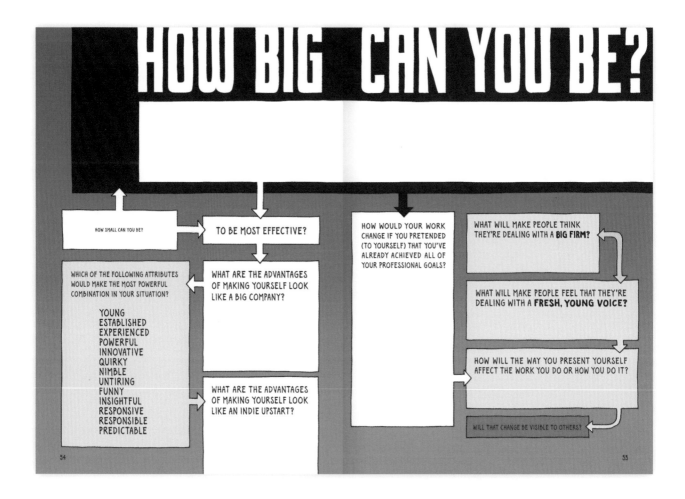

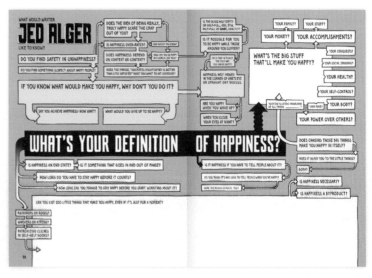

344 Questions:
Various pages,
designed and written
by Stefan Bucher

344 Questions:
Various pages,
designed and written
by Stefan Bucher.

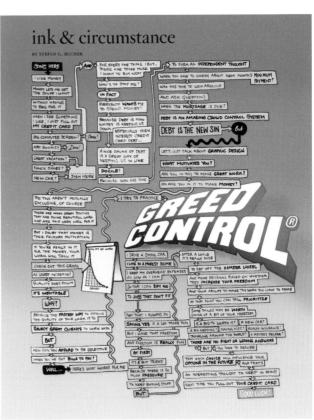

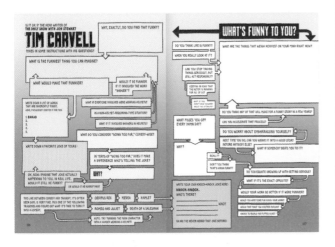

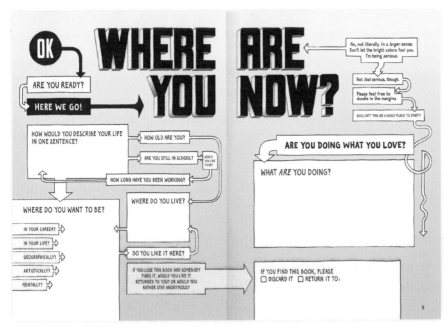

CASE STUDY:
"ALL THE NEWS THAT FITS"

⫸ PAULA SCHER

Paula Scher is always augmenting accepted form, busting convention, shifting shape, subverting style, and challenging perceptions. A clever writer with a talent for turning a phrase rather than only writing in a conventional manner, she incorporates her texts with images through typographic and lettering compositions designed to grab attention. Sometimes she uses type: "The 50 Ways I procrastinated…before designing this page" is a satiric essay by any other name. Other times she applies her handwriting and handwritten lettering.

"All the News That Fits," a visual/text essay for *Print* magazine, is a serious commentary on "the tone and tenor of the news" produced in a diary or sketchbook form. Through a collection of generic headlines during the year 2001, hand-scrawled along a timeline, Scher reveals that the top stories of the day were always held together by a diet of sex and scandal, until the events of 9/11, when precipitously, and for the following year, the underpinning was terror, until 2003 when war filled the pages.

Scher's concept could easily have been written as a narrative, but it would have lost the impact. The aggressive nature of the writing combined with the violent use of colored pencil is a barometer for the various emotions stirred by news in the post-9/11 period.

↑ *Shock and Awe,* 2005
Design: Paula Scher/Pentagram.

↓ *Procrastination* illustration for *Real Simple* magazine, 2011
Designed by Paula Scher/Pentagram

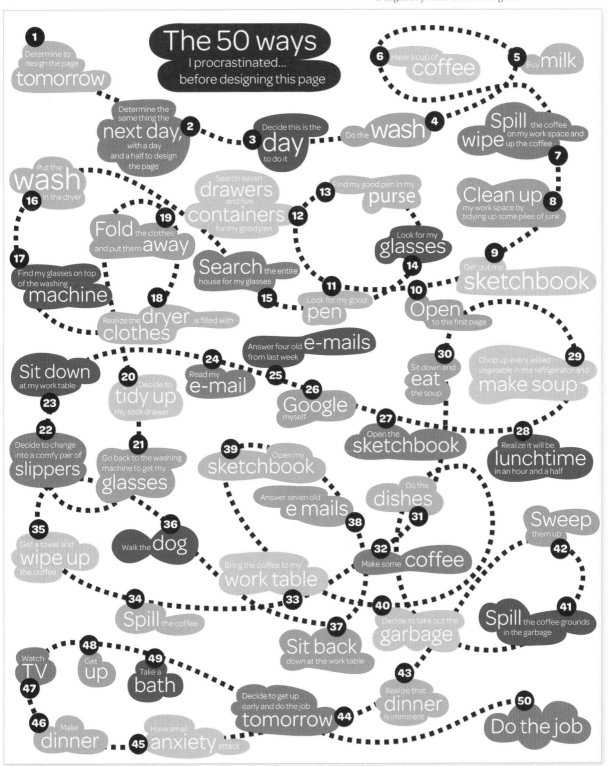

ALL THE NEWS THAT FITS

For at least a decade, I've noticed that the tone and tenor of the news sounds pretty much the same, regardless of what's going on. There is never any negative space in the news. The news always expands to fill its given format. Stories repeat in a background hum to fill dead air. If news stories are new and serious, the hum gets louder and more specific as bigger stories crowd out smaller stories. But the formats are always the same size.

After 9/11 the news abruptly switched from a background of sex to a background of terror, without missing a beat.

The following diary demonstrates the news from January 2001 through August 2003.

PAULA SCHER
NEW YORK

Shock and Awe, 2005
Design: Paula Scher/Pentagram

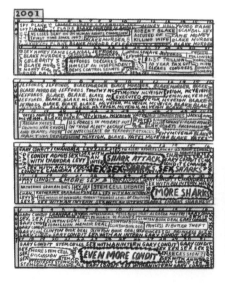

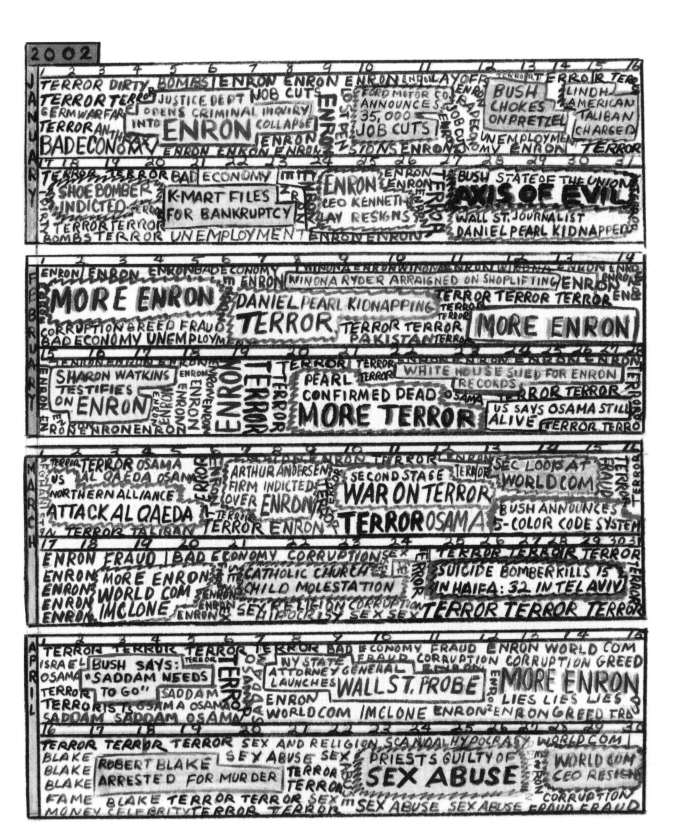

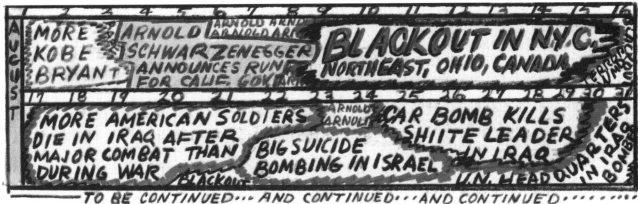

TO BE CONTINUED ··· AND CONTINUED ··· AND CONTINUED ······

CASE STUDY:
EAMES WORDS

➤➤➤ **ANDREW BYROM**

British-born Andrew Byrom makes monumental thoughts out of monumental words. Here, at A+D Museum Los Angeles, Eames Words was an exhibition that showcased the ideas—rather than the creations—of the pioneering designers Charles and Ray Eames. Organized and designed by a large creative team that was headed by Deborah Sussman (an Eames office alumna who was a founder of the design firm Sussman/Prejza), Byrom, and Todd Erlandson and Lara Hoad of the LA architecture studio (M)Arch, the show is laden with quotations that impart wisdom large and small.

Inspired by *100 Quotes by Charles Eames*, a book edited by Carla Hartman and Charles's grandson Eames Demetrios, Sussman conceived the idea of covering the walls, columns, and floor with typography, and Byrom designed the big "Eames" lettering that wraps the museum's Wilshire Boulevard façade. Erlandson suggested extending the Es into the exhibition space by turning them into display fixtures.

The Eameses' words are just as potent in the twenty-first century as they were in the twentieth; their insights transcend style, with timeless quotes such as "Take your pleasures seriously," "Beyond the age of information is the age of choices," or "You can tell more about a country from its bread and soup than you can from its museums and concert halls."

Byrom's favorites are "Toys are not really as innocent as they look" and "The Jeep, now, that's an automobile America should be proud of."

These quotations typify the couple's belief that design enhances life's simple pleasures. They also serve as the philo-sophical underpinning for the Eames-designed objects that are included in the exhibition across the street at the Los Angeles County Museum of Art, "California Design, 1930–1965: Living in a Modern Way." Together, the two exhibitions present a well-rounded picture of the Eameses' ideas and the optimism and innovation of postwar California design.

Lettering by Andrew Byrom
Photography by Clark Dugger.

the uncommon beauty
of common things ...

For an example of how limitation
works in the creative process,
consider a sculptor attacking granite with hand tools.

Granite resists such attack violently;
it is a hard material,

**It is not easy to do something good,
but it is extremely difficult to do something bad**

EPILOGUE:

IS ANYBODY READING?

Determining how many people actually read your words was once difficult. In today's media world, analytics reign supreme. If you publish online you are only a few clicks away from learning almost everything you need to know about who, where, when, and for how long your readers have engaged with your work. Or, for that matter, whether you even have any readers. Visits, hits, page clicks, and bounce backs are all considered as the measures of success or failure. In addition, social media encourages users to discuss or critique your work. So you not only know whether anyone is reading, but you also know what they think about it. Like? Dislike? How many stars?

And what about entrepreneurial sites, such as Kickstarter. com? Your finished work is less relevant than your stunning proposals. Crowd sourcing encourages but can also discourage the creative act.

All this media attention can make an instant star or abject failure out of every one of us. If your work does not appeal to your proposed niche, fuggedaboutit!

There is a lesson for the future to be learned here. And since I prefer to look at the silver lining, I refuse to sound the death knell of tradition. Rather, all this attention—or overload, if you prefer—has a clear benefit. Despite warnings that our collective attention span is microscopically reduced or our attention deficit disorder is telescopically increased (as I sit at my computer incessantly clicking the Get Mail button to the right of my three open Word files), arguably more is being written, more is being read, more is being learned than ever before.

This surplus—deluge, if you prefer—demands one thing: For a reader to invest his time (and free up brain storage space), the writing must be fluid, accessible, and enjoyable to read. Most important, the content—the research, ideas, and story—must be worthy of being read. This is not, to borrow a real estate term, a "writer's market." It is a "reader's market." The writer must "sell" the audience. And the audience must be discerning.

Is anyone reading? Everyone is, in some form and in various platforms. But as the writer, you must work extra hard to win their attention, if not their loyalty.

SELECTED BIBLIOGRAPHY

The following are informative and inspiring books that will serve as models for design writing and research. But before reading these, essential reading is *The Elements of Style* by William Strunk Jr. and E.B. White (Longman, 1999), the classic inspirational and instructional book on writing.

Albrect, Donald, Ellen Lupton, and Steven Holt. *Design Culture Now: National Design Triennial.* New York: Princeton Architectural Press, 2000.

Barringer, David. *There's Nothing Funny About Design.* New York: Princeton Architectural Press, 2009.

Bierut, Michael, et al. (Eds.). *Looking Closer: Critical Writings on Graphic Design.* New York: Allworth, 1994.

Bringhurst, Robert. *The Elements of Typographic Style.* Vancouver: Hartley & Marks, 2004.

Brody, David, and Hazel Clark (Eds.). *Design Studies: A Reader.* London: Berg Publishers, 2009.

Caplan, Ralph. *By Design: Why There Are No Locks on the Bathroom Doors in the Hotel Louis XIV and Other Object Lessons* / Edition 2. New York: Fairchild Books, 2004.

Caplan, Ralph. *Cracking the Whip: Essays on Design and Its Side Effects.* New York: Fairchild Books, 2005.

Glaser, Milton. *Drawing Is Thinking.* New York: Overlook Hardcover, 2008.

Glaser, Milton. *In Search of the Miraculous or One Thing Leads to Another.* New York: Overlook Duckworth, 2012.

Helfand, Jessica. *Screen: Essays on Graphic Design, New Media, and Visual Culture.* New York: Princeton Architectural Press, 2004.

Heller, Steven. *Design Literacy* (Second Edition). New York: Allworth Press, 2004.

Heller, Steven (Ed.). *The Education of a Graphic Designer* (Second Edition). New York: Allworth Press, 2005.

Heller, Steven. *The Graphic Design Reader.* New York: Allworth Press, 2002.

Heller, Steven. *Paul Rand.* London: Phaidon Press Ltd., 1999.

Heller, Steven, and Louise Fili. *Stylepedia: A Guide to Graphic Design Mannerisms, Quirks, and Conceits.* San Francisco: Chronicle, 2006.

Heller, Steven. *Teaching Graphic Design: Course Offerings and Class Projects from the Leading Graduate and Undergraduate Programs.* New York: Allworth Press, 2003.

Hollis, Richard. *Graphic Design: A Concise History,* Second Edition. New York/London: (World of Art) Thames and Hudson, 2001.

SELECTED BIBLIOGRAPHY

Hollis, Richard. *Swiss Graphic Design: The Origins and Growth of an International Style, 1920–1965.* New Haven: Yale University Press, 2006.

Lange, Alexandra. *Writing About Architecture: Mastering the Language of Buildings and Cities.* New York: Princeton Architectural Press, 2012.

Lupton, Ellen. *Mixing Messages: Graphic Design in Contemporary Culture.* New York: Cooper-Hewitt National Design Museum, Smithsonian Institution and Princeton Architectural Press, 1996.

Lupton, Ellen, and Abbot Miller. *Design, Writing Research: Writing on Graphic Design.* London: Phaidon Press Limited, 1999.

Lupton, Ellen. *Thinking with Type: A Critical Guide for Designers, Writers, Editors and Students.* New York: Princeton Architectural Press, 2004.

Maeda, John. *Maeda @ Maeda.* New York: Rizzoli, 2000.

Mau, Bruce. *Life Style.* New York: Phaidon Press, 2000.

Meggs, Philip B., and Alston Purvis. *A History of Graphic Design*, Fifth Edition. New York: John Wiley & Sons, 2012.

Poynor, Rick. *Designing Pornotopia: Travels in Visual Culture.* New York: Princeton Architectural Press, 2006.

Poynor, Rick. *No More Rules: Graphic Design and Postmodernism.* New Haven, CT: Yale University Press, 2003.

Poynor, Rick. *Obey The Giant.* Basel: Birkhauser Verlag, 2007.

Poynor, Rick. *Uncanny: Surrealism and Graphic Design.* Brno: Moravská Galerie, 2010.

Purcell, Kerry William. *Alexey Brodovitch.* London & New York: Phaidon Press, 2002.

Purcell, Kerry William. *Josef Müller-Brockmann.* London & New York: Phaidon Press, 2006.

Sagmeister, Stefan, and Peter Hall. *Made You Look.* New York: Booth-Clibborn, 2001.

Shaughnessy, Adrian. *How to Be a Graphic Designer Without Losing Your Soul.* New York: Princeton Architectural Press, 2005.

Shedroff, Nathan. *Design Is the Problem: The Future of Design Must be Sustainable.* Brooklyn: Rosenfeld Media, 2009.

Scher, Paula. *Make It Bigger.* New York: Princeton Architectural Press, 2002.

Thomson, Ellen M. *The Origins of Graphic Design in America.* New Haven, CT: Yale University Press, 1997.

Twemlow, Alice. *What Is Graphic Design For?* London: Rotovision, 2006.

CONTRIBUTOR BIOGRAPHIES

SEAN ADAMS is a partner at AdamsMorioka. He is a professor at Art Center College of Design, and president ex officio of AIGA.

GAIL ANDERSON is a designer, teacher, and writer. Formerly creative director of design at SpotCo and senior art director at *Rolling Stone* magazine, she is coauthor, with Steven Heller, of six design books, including *New Ornamental Type*. She is the recipient of the 2008 AIGA Medal for Lifetime Achievement.

SUE APFELBAUM is a freelance writer and editor with a focus on design, art, music, film, and culture. From 2006 to 2012 she was the editorial director for AIGA, publishing critical, inspirational, and educational content about design on the AIGA website and developing programming for AIGA's webinars.

DAVID BARRINGER is the author of *American Mutt Barks in the Yard* (Emigre, 2005) and *There's Nothing Funny About Design* (Princeton Architectural Press, 2009). He teaches design and writing at Winthrop University and MICA. Visit www.davidbarringer.com.

STEFAN G. BUCHER is the man behind 344 Design and the creator of Dailymonster.com. His latest book is *344 Questions: The Creative Person's Do-It-Yourself Guide to Insight, Survival, and Artistic Fulfillment.*

AKIKO BUSCH writes about design, culture, and the natural world for a variety of publications. She is the author of *Geography of Home: Writings on Where We Live* and *The Uncommon Life of Common Objects: Essays on Design and the Everyday*. Her most recent book of essays, *Nine Ways to Cross a River*, a collection of essays about swimming across U.S. rivers, was published in 2007.

ANDREW BYROM served a five-year apprenticeship in a North England shipyard before leaving to study graphic design in London. He is currently a professor at California State University, Long Beach, and divides his time between teaching, playing with his three children, and designing for clients including the *New York Times*, Sagmeister Inc., Penguin Books, and UCLA Extension.

RALPH CAPLAN, author of *By Design* and *Cracking the Whip*, has been a writer on design and related subjects for more than fifty years. He intends to keep at it until he gets it right.

ALLAN CHOCHINOV is the editor-in-chief of *Core77*, and the chair of the MFA Products of Design Program at the School of Visual Arts, New York.

SEYMOUR CHWAST is a founding partner of the celebrated Push Pin Studios, whose distinct style has had a worldwide influence on contemporary visual communications. In 1985 the studio's name was changed to The Pushpin Group, of which he is the director. He and Push Pin were honored at the Louvre in Paris in a two-month retrospective exhibition titled *The Push Pin Style*.

LIZ DANZICO is chair and cofounder of the MFA Interaction Design program at the School of Visual Arts, New York. She is part educator, part designer, and part editor, who writes part of her time at Bobulate.com.

MICHAEL DOOLEY is a creative director, writer and *Print* magazine contributing editor. He teaches graphic design history at Art Center, LMU, and UCLA Extension. He is the coauthor of *The Education of a Comics Artist* (Allworth Press) and *Teaching Motion Design* (Allworth Press).

MICHAEL GRANT is the director of communication at the School of Visual Arts, New York. He has held leadership roles in marketing and communications for the visual and performing arts since the late 1990s.

DEBORAH HUSSEY is a New York–based editor and writer specializing in art and art-related topics. She is the author of *Monumental: The Reimagined World of Kevin O'Callaghan* and recently completed editing a book on advanced problems in fine-art appraisal. She is board president of Enki Education.

AARON KENEDI is the FORMER editor-in-chief of *Print*, where he was responsible for developing the content for the award-winning magazine, the book division, design events, and two digital properties (including *Imprint*).

LINDA KING is a lecturer in design history, theory, and visual communication at the Institute of Art, Design and Technology, Dublin, Ireland.

BETH KLEBER is the archivist for the Milton Glaser Design Study Center and the School of Visual Arts Archives, which she helped found in 2006. The Archives contain work from distinguished designers and illustrators including Milton Glaser, Ivan Chermayeff and Tom Geismar, Henry Wolf, Seymour Chwast, James McMullan, Heinz Edelmann, George Tscherny, and Tony Palladino.

ANDREA LANGE is an architecture and design critic whose work has appeared in *Dwell*, *Print*, *New York Magazine*, and the *New York Times*. In 2012, Princeton Architectural Press published her second book, *Writing About Architecture: Mastering the Language of Buildings and Cities*.

PHIL PATTON is the author of more than a dozen books, writes about design for the *New York Times*, and has been curator of several museum shows, including *Different Roads*, at the Museum of Modern Art in New York. He teaches in the Design Criticism Program of the School of Visual Arts, New York.

MARIA POPOVA (@brainpicker) is the founder and editor of BrainPickings.org, an inventory of cross-disciplinary curiosity. She writes for *Wired UK*, The *Atlantic*, *Nieman Journalism Lab*, and *Design Observer*, among others, and is an MIT Futures of Entertainment Fellow.

EMILY POTTS is senior acquisitions editor at Rockport Publishers and content editor for RockPaperInk, Inspiration, Ideas & Opinions from Design Fanatics (www.rockpaperink.com).

RICK POYNOR is a writer, critic, lecturer, and curator specializing in design, media, and visual culture. He founded *Eye*, cofounded *Design Observer*, and contributes columns to *Eye* and Print. His latest book is *Uncanny: Surrealism and Graphic Design*.

KERRY WILLIAM PURCELL is a lecturer in design history at The University of Hertfordshire. His publications include *Alexey Brodovitch* (Phaidon Press, 2002) and *Josef Müller-Brockmann* (2006). He writes for various magazines and is also completing a Ph.D. on the role of biography in graphic design history.

STEFAN SAGMEISTER, author of *Made You Look* (reprint: Abrams, 2009) and *Things I Have Learned in My Life So Far* (Abrams, 2008), has created eye-catching graphics for clients including the Rolling Stones and Lou Reed. Solo exhibitions of Sagmeister's work have been mounted all over the world. He teaches in the MFA Design/Designer as Author + Entrepreneur department of the School of Visual Arts, New York, and has been appointed as the Frank Stanton Chair at the Cooper Union School of Art, New York.

PAULA SCHER has been a principal in the New York office of the international design consultancy Pentagram since 1991. She began her career as an art director at CBS Records in the 1970s and early 1980s, when her eclectic approach to typography became highly influential. In the mid-1990s her identity for The Public Theater fused high and low, and her recent architectural collaborations have reimagined the urban landscape as a dynamic environment of dimensional graphic design.

ELLEN SHAPIRO is a graphic designer and writer based in Irvington, New York. She is the author of two books on graphic design and a highly graphic manual and collection of multisensory materials for teaching children, especially children with learning differences, how to read. A contributing editor of *Print* magazine and *Communication Arts* magazine, she develops, photographs, write, and assembles monthly posts for *Imprint*, *Print's* blog. Her writing can also be found on Salon.com and on http://dig-it-blog.com.

ADRIAN SHAUGHNESSY is a designer, writer, publisher, and broadcaster. He is a senior tutor (graphic design) at the Royal College of Art, London.

ALEXANDER TOCHILOVSKY is the curator at the Herb Lubalin Study Center of Design and Typography at The Cooper Union. He teaches typography at The Cooper Union School of Art and is the co-owner of The Studio of ME/AT together with Mike Essl.

ALICE TWEMLOW is the chair of the SVA MFA in Design Criticism, New York, and a Ph.D. candidate in design history at the Royal College of Art, London. She writes about design for publications including *Design Observer* and *Bloomberg*, and authored the book *What Is Graphic Design For?*

VERONIQUE VIENNE was a magazine art director in the United States when she began to write to better analyze and understand the work of graphic designers, illustrators, and photographers. Today she writes books and conducts workshops on design criticism as a creative tool.

ALISSA WALKER is a Los Angeles-based design writer focused on finding innovative ways to increase public awareness and social relevance for the work of designers, architects, and other authors of visual culture. In 2010 she was named a USC Annenberg Getty Arts Journalism Fellow for her writing on design and urbanism.

INDEX